GHOST TOWNS

YESTERDAY & TODAY™

Gary B. Speck

WEST SIDE PUBLISHING

Gary B. Speck has been exploring, writing about, and photographing
ghost towns since 1968. His monthly column, "Ghost Town USA,"
has appeared in *Western & Eastern Treasures* magazine for more than 25 years.
He is the author of the book *Dust in the Wind—A Guide to American Ghost Towns*.
Television credits include programs on CNN and The History Channel.
His Web site is: http://freepages.history.rootsweb.ancestry.com/~gtusa/index.htm.

Facts verified by **Marty Strasen**

Front cover: Bodie, California

Yesterday & Today is a trademark of Publications International, Ltd.

West Side Publishing is a division of Publications International, Ltd.

Louis Weber, CEO
Publications International, Ltd.
7373 North Cicero Avenue
Lincolnwood, Illinois 60712

Permission is never granted for commercial purposes.

ISBN-13: 978-1-60553-424-4
ISBN-10: 1-60553-424-2

Manufactured in China.

8 7 6 5 4 3 2 1

Library of Congress Control Number: 2009938057

Located east of California's Sierra Nevada Mountains and north of Mono Lake, Bodie, California, is considered America's best ghost town.

Contents

GHOST TOWNS
of North America

14. Silverton, Colorado
15. Southeast Colorado Farm Towns
16. Bisbee, Arizona
17. Goldroad and Oatman, Arizona
18. Superior, Arizona
19. Vulture Mine, Arizona
20. Chloride, New Mexico
21. Lake Valley, New Mexico
22. Mogollón, New Mexico
23. Route 66 Ghosts in Texas
24. Thurber, Texas

THE NORTHWESTERN STATES

25. Bodie, Washington
26. Molson, Washington
27. Nighthawk, Washington
28. Golden, Oregon
29. Hardman, Oregon
30. Bonanza, Idaho
31. Chesterfield, Idaho
32. Silver City, Idaho
33. Elkhorn, Montana
34. Garnet, Montana
35. Granite, Montana
36. Bosler, Wyoming
37. Fort Laramie, Wyoming
38. Keeline/Jay Em, Wyoming

THE AMERICAN HEARTLAND

39. Farm Towns of North Dakota
40. The Black Hills of South Dakota
41. McGrew, Nebraska
42. Englewood, Kansas
43. Foss, Oklahoma
44. Picher, Oklahoma
45. Frontenac, Minnesota
46. Grasston Area, Minnesota

47. Dead Farm Towns in Southwestern Iowa
48. Ayrshire, Iowa
49. Galena, Illinois
50. Old Shawneetown, Illinois
51. Victoria, Michigan

THE NORTHEASTERN STATES

52. Centralia, Pennsylvania
53. Hopewell Furnace, Pennsylvania
54. Batsto, New Jersey
55. Point Lookout, Maryland
56. Kaymoor, West Virginia
57. Thurmond, West Virginia

THE SOUTHEASTERN STATES

58. Appomattox Court House, Virginia
59. Jamestown, Virginia
60. Barthell and Blue Heron, Kentucky
61. Cahawba, Alabama
62. Auraria, Georgia
63. Bulowville, Florida

HAWAII, ALASKA, AND WESTERN CANADA

64. Leper Colonies of Hawaii
65. Independence Mine, Alaska
66. Kennicott, Alaska
67. Skagway, Alaska
68. Dawson City, Yukon Territory
69. Barkerville, British Columbia
70. Fort Rodd, British Columbia
71. Dorothy and the Drumheller Valley, Alberta

THE SOUTHWESTERN STATES

1. Bodie, California
2. Darwin, California
3. Randsburg, California
4. Salton Sea, California
5. Belmont, Nevada
6. Gold Point, Nevada
7. Rhyolite, Nevada
8. Grafton, Utah
9. The Tintic, Utah
10. Topaz, Utah
11. Animas Forks, Colorado
12. Nevadaville, Colorado
13. St. Elmo, Colorado

What Is a Ghost Town?

Boom then Bust.

A town is born.

A living town dies.

A ghost town is created.

Ghost town: "a once-flourishing town wholly or nearly deserted usu. as a result of the exhaustion of some natural resource."

—Merriam-Webster's New Collegiate Dictionary

[By permission. From *Merriam-Webster's Collegiate® Dictionary, 11th Edition*©2009 by Merriam-Webster, Incorporated (www.Merriam-Webster.com).]

Popular opinion maintains that a ghost town is a long, dusty street lined with ragtag buildings in various stages of decay. Signs are falling off storefronts, glassless windows are framed with tattered curtains flapping in the breeze, and squeaky doors slap against wooden doorframes. Tumbleweeds bounce and roll down Main Street, piling in rows against the curling, chocolate-brown, wood-batten siding of rickety structures. Boot Hill epitaphs decorate granite and marble head-stones, telling tales of gun smoke and boot leather, while the names and dates of the departed were long ago sandblasted free of battered wooden headboards and crosses. In saloons, thick dust coats the once smooth bar surface while empty bottles garnish the back bar. The evidence of a miner's last card game lies strewn across the desiccated gaming table in the corner. Only ghosts remain.

Fact Vs. Fiction

That's the romanticized version, but here come some solid facts. In the larger scheme of things, the United States of America is a young country. Yet it probably has a higher concentration of ghost towns than anywhere else in the world. These towns range in time from the earliest days of settlement in the country during the early 1600s to as recently as yesterday. The vast majority of such towns, however, date from between the 1850s and the 1950s.

Why is that? Was it restlessness, zest for exploring new territory, or "Manifest Destiny" that motivated Americans to head west, to occupy the continent from sea to shining sea? That slow, somewhat orderly flow of civilization west was interrupted by a singular event—a world-changing event. In fact,

Sitting in the low mountains just east of Death Valley, the Nevada desert closes in on the gaunt ruins of a dead city. Thousands of people caught up in an early-1900s gold frenzy thronged the streets of Rhyolite, where today only lizards scamper and rattlesnakes coil in the scant shade. The once magnificent John S. Cook Bank building—and the entire city—now looks like a post-apocalyptic idea out of a Hollywood movie. This is no movie set, however, it is real. And it is dead.

A bakery wagon pauses along the road out of Nevadaville, Colorado, in 1889, while others go about their business. Today, this town's commercial and population centers are nearly gone, mere memories of the days when prosperity reigned here.

three simple words—"Gold in California"—created a worldwide clamor to reach that distant shore. "California or Bust" was the new slogan. Gold for the picking was the motivation.

Would-be miners converged on California by the tens of thousands: by ship, by foot, and by wagon. A completely new national mind-set developed. Roots were forgotten, and instant towns founded on a single, unstable economy mushroomed all over the state, quickly spreading as the mining excitement waned, running out of California's mountains and spreading north and east into the hinterlands.

As time marched on, scores of thousands of towns were established and then abandoned; either that or they faded greatly as their economies failed. Each of these now ghosted towns were once living communities of people, each pursuing individual hopes and dreams, working long hours to provide food for the table, putting down roots in new land, and just trying to get ahead. They toiled in mines, on farms, or in forests. They built railroads, river ports, and massive industrial complexes. They all contributed to the building of the United States—no different than Americans today, except without computers, digital music, microwave ovens, or SUVs.

What caused these towns to fade or die? It was often as simple as the failure of the single economic support for the town, such as a mine petering out. Other towns were established along transportation corridors with the intent of snagging a railroad line, highway crossroads, or the county seat. But intent and reality often differed, and the railroad missed the town by miles, the crossroads were established elsewhere, or the county-seat honors were awarded to another town across the county.

Nature has also contributed to the formation of ghost towns. Settlements were often established in river bottoms to allow their development as a river port. The very reason they were established there, however, sometimes caused their demise in the form of flooding. Other towns were built in different inhospitable or borderline locations subject to natural disasters or other acts of nature.

Another, more recent creator of ghost towns is the usurpation of land by the government for something beyond that land's original use. Forts and military bases often expanded, causing towns to be either moved or absorbed. Testing facilities and weapons development plants sometimes required huge tracts of land, which caused eviction of communities. The creation of reservoirs also resulted in relocation or abandonment of entire towns. Environmental disasters of human origin caused by chemical contamination have resulted in the vacating of numerous areas. And in America's agricultural regions, massive, mechanized, corporate farms decreased the need for tiny towns to support mom-and-pop farms—and as a double whammy, those same towns are economically frozen out by big-box retailers establishing themselves in larger, more stable towns nearby.

A Historical Legacy

Ghost towns are American history. Unfortunately, those with tangible remains are rapidly deteriorating, falling victim to the elements and humanity's less than desirable

whims, vanishing like dust in the wind. Visiting these wonderful relics of Americana gives one a glimpse of the hopes and dreams of folks from the not-too-distant past, a past that each citizen needs to help preserve for the future.

Encompassing all of the above information, perhaps a better definition of a ghost town varies slightly from Merriam-Webster: "Ghost town: a town or community that at one time had a commercial or population center and is either wholly abandoned or has faded greatly from its peak, now just a shadow of its former self."

What is a ghost town? Read on. . . .

Nestled in its colorful Colorado mountain bowl, the former silver-mining town of Silverton is just an echo of its previous incarnation. Where 3,000 people once roamed, just a tad more than 500 remain in this historic old county seat today.

The aroma of fresh-baked pies has been replaced by the dusty smell of well-seasoned wood in Animas Forks, Colorado. Mournful breezes blow where the joyful sounds of children playing once echoed through this vacant home in the Southwestern mountains. Dead window sockets glare eerily where glassed-in windows once glowed with warmth. One hundred years ago, this house was alive. Today, it is a rickety skeleton of the past.

The Southwestern States

"This day some kind of mettle was found in the tail race that looks like goald first discovered by James Martial, the Boss of the Mill." That was the entry in prospector Henry Bigler's diary for Monday, January 24, 1848. And so it began. On that cold morning, James Marshall, the foreman of a sawmill plopped on the bank of California's American River, changed U.S. history. Walking along the mill's tailrace, he plucked a pea-size nugget of gold out of the gravel, effectively firing the starting gun for the world's greatest treasure hunt. Despite initial attempts to stifle the news, word spread. *Gold! Gold in California!*

In a very measured understatement during his State of the Union address on December 5, 1848, President James K. Polk tossed kindling onto the flames of the burgeoning case of worldwide gold fever.

"The accounts of the abundance of gold in that territory are of such an extraordinary character as would scarcely command belief were they not corroborated by the authentic reports of officers in the public service who have visited the mineral district and derived the facts which they detail from personal observation.

"... Nearly the whole of the male population of the country have gone to the gold districts. Ships arriving on the coast are deserted by their crews and their voyages suspended for want of sailors."

Newspapers splashed golden headlines to the far corners of the earth—the California Gold Rush was under way. In a five-year span, some 300,000 argonauts from all over the world descended upon the soon to become "Golden State." Few got rich, but all had a grand adventure.

Gold Fever!

From 1848 to 1853, the rush for gold was in full boom. Lots of gold was found—some 12 million ounces, worth multiple billions in today's dollars. The once-pastoral western landscape was converted into teeming clusters of temporary mining camps and transitory towns with little thought given to permanence. Once the riches were stripped from the rivers, the miners moved on, leaving behind remains of the ephemeral camps and towns, the people taking only what they could carry or toss into a wagon or on the back of a mule or horse.

In what barely seemed any time at all, California's rivers had given up their treasure, and the easy diggings were gone. The gold mining industry itself, however,

Visions of wealth drove prospectors across the region's mountains and deserts in search of gold, silver, and other valuable mineral deposits. When pay dirt was found, as it was in Silver City, Utah (*pictured*), the discoveries were often quickly followed by a rush of people, all looking to cash in on the find. Saloon owners, teamsters, hoteliers, blacksmiths, storekeepers, and people of many legitimate (as well as nefarious) trades converged on the site, slapping together an instant town.

was firmly entrenched as less people-intensive hydraulic and hard-rock mining took over. Many of the original argonauts morphed into prospectors, now spreading east and north across the West looking for the next boom. New discoveries were made. And new mining rushes ensued.

Outside the original gold mining region in California, prospectors combed the Great Basin, the deserts, and even the Rocky Mountain forests in Nevada, Utah, Colorado, Arizona, New Mexico—all the way to Texas—in search of golden wealth. And gold was found. So were silver, copper, and a plethora of other valuable minerals.

Towns boomed and busted. The prospectors then moved on to the next "Big Thing."

This was a cycle that repeated over and over and over again. Where viable communities remained, agriculture, transportation, and government followed. Mining opened up the American Southwest, creating the vast majority of the thousands of towns scattered across the region's landscape. Rising and ebbing across the economic landscape, farming, cattle, logging, and railroad building also tossed in their contributions, as did tourism and the military.

Abandoned to the Elements

Today, most of these towns are gone or empty—at best, they are mere shells of what they once had been. Ghost towns, they are barren or rubbled sites with a few foundation outlines, crumbled piles of rock, or melted adobe walls. Some—such as Belmont, Nevada; Chloride, New Mexico; and Darwin, California—have a smattering of ruins, abandoned buildings, and a small resident population. Others have survived and are still living, although not thriving. The population of places such as Randsburg, California; Nevadaville, Colorado; and Oatman, Arizona, is much lower than during their boom days. A select few towns such as Bisbee, Arizona, and Silverton, Colorado, remain viable communities and the seats of their respective counties. Even so, population levels are far below what they had been in the boom years, and these communities are filled with historic structures.

Because most of the land in the Southwest is dry, aridity has preserved the majority of structures. Government ownership of many towns hasn't created an economic reason to tear down unused buildings (the government doesn't pay property taxes to itself). The American Southwest is truly a place where well-preserved ghost towns still give travelers a glimpse of the past.

The rugged landscape of the American West can inspire conflicting emotions. This is the land where a little girl was supposedly overheard praying, "Goodbye God, I'm going to Bodie." Of course, the Bodie newspaper refuted that, claiming she was misquoted. The quote should have read, "Good. By God, I'm going to Bodie." The West is where Billy the Kid, Black Bart, the Earp brothers, Mark Twain, and hundreds of legendary characters roamed—good, bad and in-between. It is the land of 20-mule teams, Wells Fargo and Company stagecoaches, and Route 66.

In this land of vast horizons, sagebrush, and majestic scenery, thousands of ghost towns are eager to share their stories.

Explorers and pioneers pushing against the edges of civilization discovered gold, silver, and other precious minerals in scattered areas across the American Southwest. Towns such as Bodie, California (*above*), grew quickly and were then abandoned once mine production dipped below the profitability line. When these communities died, people left behind their withered hopes and faded dreams.

What remains today are weather-worn schools, churches, businesses, and homes. Unpainted wooden buildings have seasoned into a deep brown. Adobe, rock, and brick structures are crumbling. Throughout the Southwest, picturesque abandonment abounds as a quiet legacy to a boisterous past.

Bodie, California

Yesterday's Bodie was a true boomtown filled with a couple thousand wooden buildings and as many as 10,000 people milling through its bustling streets. Today's Bodie is a state historic park, a gaunt skeleton of what once was: the best-known, most-written about, and most-photographed ghost town in America. Killings were a daily occurrence, and "The Bad Man from Bodie" became legend.

Waterman S. (Bill) Bodey discovered gold east of the Sierras and north of Mono Lake in 1859. He perished in a snowstorm that winter, but a small, quiet mining camp named after him developed at the discovery site. The peacefulness changed in 1875, however, with the exposure of a massive, rich pocket of gold deep in one of the mines. Bodie became *the* place to be and went from quiet to rough, uncultured, and uncivilized overnight. By 1877 the mile-long main street was solidly lined with businesses,

including 65 saloons. In 1881, a local pastor called Bodie "a sea of sin, lashed by the tempests of lust and passion."

But even before then, the glitter was fading. The mine had only so much gold, and when it was all extracted, Bodie languished and died. Two fires, in 1892 and 1932, left charred memories of any "excess" buildings that had remained after the people left. Since then, there has been no rebuilding and little restoration. What remains is lovingly maintained in a state of "arrested decay."

If you listen quietly, you can almost hear the ghosts . . .

"And now my comrades all are gone
Naught remains to toast.
They have left me here in my misery,
Like some poor wandering ghost."

The corrugated steel and wooden buildings in what may be the ultimate ghost town glow in the late afternoon sun. More than a century of horrid winters, a pair of major fires, and decades of ghosthood have destroyed about 95 percent of the town. Yet, the Bodie that remains is a real gem. About 150 weather-blasted buildings still stand, making this the best classic ghost town in the country. It's the popular stereotype that folks expect from a ghost town: Frozen in time, Bodie's heart and soul live on in this current view stretching from the wooden Methodist church on the left to the Standard Mine's corrugated metal buildings on the upper right slope.

Above: Spared from fire, a few buildings still line Bodie's gap-toothed Main Street, which now plays host to growing grass and a soulful quiet where commerce once bustled and thousands trod.

Above: In this northwest view up Green Street, a number of historic buildings mark the past. The large two-story wooden structure on the right was the school, and the brick building just beyond it was the town's power plant. At the far end of the street are the Methodist church and the big barn.

Left: Bodie has been a favorite subject for photographers for more than a century. Famed photographer Burton Frasher came to Bodie in 1927, recording the post-boom mining town for one of his postcard series. Taken from Bodie Bluff, above the Standard Mine, this photograph shows zebra-stripe snow fields behind the town that add contrast to the visible buildings, most of which were burned in the big fire of June 23, 1932.

Left: The Bunker Hill Mine, discovered in 1861, was worked on and off through multiple owners until 1874, when an underground cave-in exposed a golden bonanza. The Standard Mining Company incorporated, gold flowed out, and investor money flowed in. The complex burned in October 1898, but it was quickly rebuilt and in full operation by February 1899.

Left: Sam Leon's Bar (*on left*) and an old barber shop (*on right*) face the morning sun at the northern end of Main Street. *Above:* Even though Bodie's firehouse saw a lot of action, it was powerless against the big fires of 1892 and 1932.

Above: James Stuart Cain owned this home, as well as the Bodie Bank and the Standard Mine. During Bodie's twilight years, he purchased abandoned properties, and in 1962 the Cain family sold Bodie to the state. *Below:* Leaning almost beyond the point of no return and preserved as it was in 1962 when the state took over, this iconic outhouse sits behind the town's firehouse.

HISTORY COMES ALIVE

One of Bodie's most unique qualities is that the public is not allowed to wander inside the buildings that remain. This singular rule has kept the interiors pristine, preserving the aura of folks walking away from their homes and businesses without even clearing away the remains of their daily lives.

Above: In 1879, this international money exchange receipt, from Wells Fargo and Company, was issued to Henry Billings, likely a miner in town, payable to Maria Billings in London.

Above: Merchandise remains inside Harvey Boone's store. Boone, a direct descendant of famed frontier explorer Daniel Boone, also operated a stable and livery business. *Right:* Over the life of a mining town, businesses came and went, each business owner filled with dreams and aspirations. Over the years, this pair of buildings hosted a variety of businesses.

Above: Harvey Boone built his general store and the adjacent brick warehouse at the northwest corner of Main and Green streets in the heart of downtown Bodie in 1879. He operated it until around 1900.

Above: The Bodie School moved into this Green Street building, previously occupied by the Bon Ton Lodging House, shortly after a hooligan burnt the third school building down. *Left:* Three of Bodie's classic commercial buildings anchor the south end of Main Street. Built in 1879, the brick post office later housed the Dechambeau Hotel. Next door is the two-story wooden Independent Order of Odd Fellows (IOOF) building with its upstairs lodge and downstairs undertaker. Just right of the gap is the Miners Union Hall, which today is the Bodie Museum.

Darwin, California

The desiccated, ragtag silver-mining ghost of Darwin nestles against the bone-dry Darwin Hills, smack-dab in the middle of moonscape desert west of Death Valley. It was named after Dr. E. Darwin French, an explorer who led an 1860 prospecting trip into the desert east of the Sierras searching for the legendary Lost Gunsight lode, a supposed ledge of pure silver reportedly discovered by a California gold rush–bound argonaut. The traveler lost a rifle sight and, in searching for it, found a rich outcropping of silver ore, out of which he carved a new sight. A legend born—a ledge lost.

French's party was unsuccessful, but it did locate rich silver outcroppings at Coso, California, opening up the desert for additional discoveries. In 1874, silver-lead ore was found northeast of Coso, resulting in the mining camp named after Dr. French. By 1875, Darwin was a wild boomtown filled with saloons, a post office, saloons, hotels, saloons, restaurants, saloons, and many other businesses (including saloons). Crude and rowdy, Darwin had more than 1,000 folks in 1876. Gun fights and stage robberies were common, and they only embellished Darwin's reputation. But mining eventually slowed, labor

disputes arose, and other boomtowns beckoned. Darwin withered quickly, its citizenry scattering. By 1880, a mere six years after the town was founded, only 85 people remained.

Today, Darwin has a split personality. The original Darwin is a gap-toothed cluster of weather-beaten false fronts and shacks, interspersed with scores of dead cars, watched over by 50-some residents. Just to the north, soldier-straight rows of homes and buildings mark the Anaconda-owned company town that flourished between 1944 and 1976.

Old shop buildings remain at the Anaconda Copper Mining Company's post–World War II mining camp. Anaconda bought all the patented mines in the Darwin Hills, consolidating them as the Darwin Mines. Between August 1945 and March 1954, some 100 million pounds of lead, 44 million pounds of zinc, and 5.6 million ounces of silver were produced. As production tapered off, leasers operated the mine. Anaconda sold it in 1976, and it closed completely in 1983. The company camp and its empty buildings can still be viewed from the highway.

Above: Everyone turned out in their finest for the arrival of the stage in Darwin around 1900. Even the dog sitting between the two ladies in front of the Cosmopolitan Restaurant donned a dress bandana.

Below: Downtown Darwin's crossroads at Main Street and Market Street is marked by a cluster of ancient businesses such as The Outpost with its canopied false front, fading paint, and dead gas pumps that once dispensed Shell gasoline to travelers. This building is said to have started life in the 1920s as a pool hall before being reborn and remodeled into a café. It later served as a general store, gas station, and post office. The current post office operates out of a more recently constructed building elsewhere in town.

Left: The Darwin Dance Hall sits across Market Street to the southeast of The Outpost at the main crossroads in the heart of town. Like other buildings in Darwin, it has served numerous purposes and supported various businesses over the years, including a Miners Union Hall. It is still used as a social gathering spot for Darwin's remaining residents. Despite being gutted by major fires three times, the latest in 1918, Darwin is still a fascinating semi-ghost town filled with colorful characters and well-worn buildings interspersed with dead Airstreams, Volkswagens, and Chevrolets.

Randsburg, California

No airs here. This is the real thing, barely hangin' in there by the nails on the hands of its 77 folks (according to the 2000 census). The still-living Mojave Desert gold-mining town of Randsburg is located just a mile west of a major highway yet is overlooked by tens of thousands of bustling tourist-carrying vehicles zipping up and down U.S. Highway 395, all in a hurry to get their occupants to or from unknown destinations. Founded in 1895, Randsburg is colorful, dusty, and honest, wearing its mining heritage and resultant ambiance well. Its one-time boom is long gone, as is the 100-stamp mill, the $20 million in gold, and the 1,500 to 2,500 residents who pried it from the ground.

Butte Avenue, Randsburg's main street, is lined with century-old false fronts, a curled boardwalk, and memories of the glory days so vivid they can be photographed. The general store is still open, serving the needs of the locals and tourists alike. A couple of saloons still dispense food, drinks, and advice. And the tiny but surprisingly well-stocked museum opens its doors to the public on the weekends. Mining equipment and mine headframes decorate the town and the dry, dusty, hills that surround it.

Randsburg is a working town, not a tourist trap. Pride in the past exudes from empty storefronts that compete with each other to have their portraits taken. Be sure to stop in the general store and enjoy a delicious banana split in Southern California's town that's too tough to die!

Above: In the 1970s, these three little false fronts on the south side of Butte Avenue were packed with antiques for sale. Restoration has brought new life to these old buildings. *Left:* Randsburg's 100-stamp mill is imprinted on a 1906-era Yellow Aster Mining & Milling Company check. The Yellow Aster Mine turned down-on-their-luck prospectors Charles Burcham, John Singleton, and Frederick Mooers into millionaires. Burcham's wife, Dr. Rose Burcham, also deserves credit, as she nixed selling the discovery at the outset.

Left: Built in 1897, the original post office building later served as the Miner's Union Hall. It currently houses an art gallery.

Above: The General Store is the place to shop, as well as to meet and greet. Its 1930s-era soda fountain still offers meals, old-fashioned sodas, and malteds, all served with friendly, unpretentious charm and hospitality. Visitors can sit and jabber with residents or shop for books on local interests, maps, and magazines. *Left:* Randsburg's rambling post office currently resides in the basement of the Opera House Café, which serves food, drink, and melodramas.

Above: Weathered wood, peeling paint, rusty treasures, potted desert plants, and a welded horseshoe cactus plant create a true ghost town still life.

Above: Only missing its wooden sidewalk and batwing doors, the White House Saloon comes straight out of the Old West. *Bottom right:* The squat, concrete jail at the west end of town still greets visitors to Randsburg. Inside its single cell, a display shows what life "on the inside" was like for those unfortunate enough to sample its hospitality.

LOST TO HISTORY

Not every part of a ghost town has been carefully identified and recorded. Some buildings hold their mystery, the details of their pasts having disappeared into the mists of time. If only the spirit of this unidentified false front along the north side of upper Butte Avenue could speak, it would tell gripping tales of gold mining, of boom, and of bust.

The California Rand

FILLED WITH A handful of interesting ghost and semi-ghost towns, the Rand Mining District (aka The California Rand) straddles the line between Kern and San Bernardino counties in California's northwestern Mojave Desert. Named after South Africa's famous Witwatersrand Mining District, this area is an outgrowth of earlier, "beans-and-bacon" mining camps at Goler and Summit Dry Diggings, which are now barren sites.

Other mining towns with tangible remains in the California Rand include:

Garlock: This once-busy little mining town also served as an early milling site for Randsburg's ore. Several abandoned building shells and ruins are all that remain.

Johannesburg: This barely living town still has a few active businesses along U.S. Highway 395. It was a gold-mining town and railroad-shipping center for Randsburg ore.

Red Mountain: The desiccated remains here are all that mark a once-rip-roaring silver-mining town dating to the 1920s. In the shadow of the multimillion-dollar Kelly Silver Mine (*shown at left*), remains include mine buildings, empty stores, and saloons along Highway 395.

Atolia: The site of a frenzied rush for tungsten nodules during the World War I years can still be found in a few abandoned buildings and numerous small headframes above mine-shafts, such as the one shown here.

Salton Sea, California

This is not a ghost *town*, but a ghost *sea*. One of the most unique places in the country, the Salton Sea is also California's largest lake. It fills a sub-sea level basin almost as deep as Death Valley's famed Bad-water, and it is a basin whose only outlet is through evaporation.

The sea's history is unusual, caused by a colossal "oops" in planning for irrigation in 1905. That error allowed the rampaging Colorado River to escape its normal banks and run wild off to the north into the Salton Sink. Two years later, the river's flow was returned toward the Gulf of California, but by then California had a new lake.

Minor shoreline improvement began shortly after that, but it wasn't until 1958 that major development turned the Salton Sea into California's Riviera: a bustling fishing, boating, and recreational paradise. Salton City, Salton Sea Beach, Desert Shores, North Shore, and Bombay Beach thrived, drawing thousands of visitors daily for roughly the next 20 years.

Then came the summers of 1976 and 1977. Torrential rains from a pair of tropical storms transformed that Riviera into a memory. Resorts, marinas, and small communities ringing the sea were partially flooded or disappeared entirely into the increasingly saline waters, proof that even a one-foot water rise can have disastrous impacts in a flat desert basin.

Today, silence reigns around the shoreline of the Salton Sea, where the stinky stew of water is so salty even the fish die off by the millions every summer, and dead resorts no longer echo with the excited voices of vacationers.

Above: From the beginning of development in 1958 through the mid-1970s, Salton Sea Beach was one of several resort boomtowns touted as a wonderful place to vacation, spend weekends, or even to spend one's retirement. *Right:* Designed by architect Albert Frey, the North Shore Beach and Yacht Club opened to great fanfare in 1962. For 20 years, this resort boomed, pulling weekenders, vacationers, and Hollywood celebrities into what was labeled as Southern California's Riviera.

Today, both the North Shore Yacht Club (*above*) and the rickety Desert Shores Trailer Park and Marina dock (*below*) are abandoned shells of the glory days, both looking out over boatless marinas fronting a dying sea.

Above: After the Salton Sea flooded in 1977, the beach resort Bombay Beach lost nearly a third of its community. A dike was quickly installed to stop the encroaching waters, but those on the wrong side of the dike were in trouble. Today the sea side of the dike is a wonderland of mobile homes, abandoned stores, and the marina.

Belmont, Nevada

In his book *Preserving the Glory Days,* author and historian Shawn Hall calls Belmont "The Queen of Nye County's ghost towns."

He's right.

Once home to about 4,000 people, Belmont is just a shadow of the bustling silver mining town it once was. Founded in 1865, Belmont had—within a year—become the crazed focus of a major silver rush and a small city. In 1867, the town obtained the Nye County seat, a position it held until 1905, when Tonopah wrested the honor. But by then, Belmont was gasping for air.

In between, Belmont experienced 40 years of excitement. Due to the rich silver mines that pumped out more than $15 million, it lasted longer than most mining camps. Amenities of the town included boarding houses, a brewery, a church, a fire department, fraternal organizations, general stores, a livery stable, newspapers, restaurants, saloons, sawmills, a stage line, and an undertaker.

In 1914, Belmont's ghosts were dusted off, and the post office and mines reopened. After an eight-year run that saw another million dollars in silver added to the total production, however, they all closed again in 1922.

Today's Belmont is considerably different from the Belmont of 1880. Newer cabins dot the hillsides, and a bed-and-breakfast and an operating saloon serve those who visit. The massive brick courthouse, ruins of three ore mills, and the cemetery compete with a crumbling Main Street for attention. Along Main Street, roofless and frontless rock buildings mix with wooden buildings reduced to piles of kindling. This magnificent relic of Americana is located about an hour's drive northeast of Tonopah.

Above: Built in February 1868, the 40-stamp Combination Mill just east of Belmont crushed a good share of the $15 million in silver-lead ores produced in the area. In 1915, it was torn down; the bricks were reused to build the Cameron Mill. The tall smokestack on the right still stands (*opposite page*). *Left:* A key part of Belmont's second boom, the Cameron Mill was located about a quarter mile south of the old Combination Mill. It is often incorrectly referred to as the Highbridge Mill.

Above: Ruins and rubble mark the once-bustling heart of one of Nevada's largest silver mining towns. From 1867 through the late 1880s, dozens of stores, saloons, hotels, and other businesses competed for customers. Today's only competition in the brick, rock, and wooden ruins comes from birds, lizards, and snakes jostling each other for slivers of sun and shade.
Right: Towering high over the scrubby hillsides on the east side of Belmont, the brick smokestack and rock-walled ruins are all that remain of the once-active Combination Mill. The brick-cased opening in the lower rock wall leads to an explosives bunker.

Above: Nearly ten years after Belmont snagged the county seat from the town of Ione, its two-story brick courthouse was open, serving the county until 1905. In 1974, Nye County transferred ownership of the building to the Nevada Division of State Parks, which has begun restoration work.

Gold Point, Nevada

This is a town that has had three ruffles of excitement and three different names to go with them. First, lime was discovered in 1868, and Lime Point, a small tent mining camp, developed at the mines. In 1880, some silver was mined, but due to isolation and expensive transportation, those mines closed by 1882. But rich silver and gold discoveries made in 1905 at Tonopah, Goldfield, and Bullfrog/Rhyolite created a mining rush throughout western Nevada. Railroads were built, and older discoveries were revisited, including the Lime Point deposits.

The flame for the town was relit in 1908 with the discovery of rich horn silver. On May 16, 1908, a post office opened its doors in the brand-new boomtown of Hornsilver, which had a population of 1,000 people and more than 200 buildings and tents containing shops, stores, and at least 13 saloons. By the 1930s, however, gold outproduced silver, so on October 16, 1932, Hornsilver changed its name to Gold Point.

The end of the town came on October 8, 1942, when the War Production Board issued Limitation Order L-208, shutting down all nonessential mines for the duration of World War II. As a result, Gold Point died. By the late 1960s, this classic little ghost town had about 40 wooden buildings still standing.

Located in Esmeralda County about 30 miles southwest of Goldfield, Gold Point is owned by "Sheriff" Harold T. Stone and his partner Red Dog Lil, baby boomers who always wanted to own a ghost town. Thanks to Sheriff Stone, Gold Point is not forgotten and is being lovingly preserved and restored for all to enjoy.

One hundred years ago, a thousand folks thronged the streets of this bustling mining town whose mines produced more than a million dollars worth of silver and gold. Today, the ghosts compete for space with the handful of residents who are slowly restoring the remaining buildings.

Left: The upper part of the false front on this old structure is marked Hornsilver Townsite & Telephone Company. It is said to have been a saloon, and today it is one of several dozen still-standing buildings marking this great little ghost town. *Below:* This building, once housing Gold Point's post office (which closed in 1967), general store, and gas station, now functions as the town's museum. Attached to the store on the right is the former postmistress's home. She is said to have fallen in love with the bachelor store owner who, after they married, moved out of his bachelor pad at the rear of the store and into the house.

Above: In 1908, Hornsilver's primary street housed a long line of tent stores and crude shanties. Even so, businesses such as this bakery—offering bread, pies, and cakes for sale—brought touches of civilization to the heart of Nevada's desert.

Rhyolite, Nevada

In early 1907, Nevada's fourth largest city was a booming, modern city of about 6,000 people excitedly looking toward a golden future. Three years later, 90 percent of those folks were gone. What happened?

During August 1904, Frank "Shorty" Harris and Ernest L. "Ed" Cross discovered rich, froggy-looking gold ore. Since neither man kept quiet, within a few months their Bullfrog claim was surrounded by miners and boom camps. Just uphill, the speculative camp of Rhyolite sold its first lots in November 1904. Six months later, it had 1,500 people and streets lined with tents and wooden shanties. Bullfrog then croaked.

It didn't take long for San Francisco money to find Rhyolite. Tents and shanties turned into multistory concrete and rock buildings. Electricity, a water/sewer system, and telephones brought newborn Rhyolite into the modern era.

But at 5:12 A.M. on April 18, 1906, nature turned off the cash, devastating San Francisco by a massive earthquake. Financial aftershocks rocked the rest of the country, but Rhyolite refused to die. A year later, Rhyolite had roughly 6,000 inhabitants and a whole host of businesses befitting a city of its stature. Unfortunately, a crash was all but inevitable. No money meant bye-bye good times! In April 1910, the lights went out for the remaining 675 residents of the "city that would last a lifetime." By 1920, only 14 people lingered.

Today, the streets are quiet. Crumbling buildings are falling victim to time, vandals, and weather, while the exciting sounds of boomtown life no longer reverberate along the streets in this gaunt ghost city.

Above: Opened in June 1908, as Rhyolite was beginning to fade, the architecturally ornate passenger depot for the Las Vegas & Tonopah Railroad was one of the nicest in Nevada. Today, it's as solid as the day it was built (*opposite page*). *Below:* The Montgomery-Shoshone Mine was discovered in 1905 and purchased in early 1906 by Charles Schwab. In September 1907, the 300-ton cyanide mill (the large white building at center) began operation. The mine temporarily closed in January 1910, reopened in April, and then shut down for good in March 1911. During that short run, it produced almost two million dollars in gold. Rhyolite can be seen at right in the distance.

Left: Of unknown heritage and vintage, this wooden false front previously housed Rhyolite's government caretaker and is currently signed as the "Rhyolite Mercantile." *Below:* For a couple of years shortly after being built in 1908, the Las Vegas & Tonopah Railroad station swarmed with travelers coming and going. By 1910, however, they were mostly going. This is the only still-complete major building in town, due to the fact that it remained occupied until the 1980s. Beginning in 1937, it operated as a restaurant and casino.

Above: The magnificent ruins of the John S. Cook bank building are probably some of the most photographed ghost-town remains in Nevada. This three-story structure, constructed of reinforced concrete for about $90,000 in 1907, was built to last a lifetime. For less than three years, it was the largest building in Rhyolite, housing a bank on the first floor, a dentist and other offices on the second, and the post office in the basement. It had imported marble flooring, indoor plumbing, and electricity. Closed in early 1910, by the end of that year, it had been stripped and all the fixtures were sold at auction. Once the roof, the windows and doors, and the second floor were removed, the roofless shell began to crumble.

Above left: Tom Kelly used adobe mortar and roughly 30,000 bottles to build his bottle house. Most of those were Adolphus Busch (now know as Anheuser-Busch Breweries) beer bottles, which he probably collected from Rhyolite's numerous saloons. The only survivor of at least three bottle houses in Rhyolite, it was completed in February 1906. In 1924, the house was partially restored for a movie, and between 1936 and 1954 it served as a private residence/museum. From 1954 until 1989, it had a new owner and continued as a private residence. It was restored again in the summer of 2005. *Above:* Detritus of daily life decorates the side of the wishing well outside the bottle house. *Left:* The free Goldwell Open Air Museum sculpture park features ghostly art such as *The Last Supper.* It is located just off the entry road into Rhyolite.

EASY COME, EASY GO

In the early 1900s, merchants and brothers Hyram D. and Lyman D. Porter ran a successful business in the Southern California mining town of Randsburg. Wind of the boom at Rhyolite caught their attention, so they packed up some goods and checked out both Beatty and Rhyolite. In April 1905, the Porter Brothers opened their Rhyolite store in a tent and within two months relocated to a wood-frame building. A year later, they were housed in this magnificent Golden Street rock building with a cut-stone front and a pair of large plate glass show windows. There they sold almost everything except liquor. The brothers also had a warehouse and lumberyard. In May 1910, they liquidated their holdings and closed the store. Hyram D. Porter remained as the postmaster until the post office was discontinued in September 1919.

Above: Built with a $20,000 bond, the two-story school was erected with reinforced concrete in 1908. The last major building to be built in Rhyolite, it was a new school, replacing the first, a typical wooden one-room building that had been blown off its foundation. Three classrooms were located downstairs and one upstairs, along with an auditorium. The roof, the second floor, fixtures, and all wooden parts were taken to Beatty, Nevada, when the middle school there was built. And the bond? It was paid off in the 1970s, 50 years after the school closed!

Grafton, Utah

The massive tan-and-red-striped cliffs of Zion National Park stand guard over an idyllic setting where only weathered split-rail fencing, green canopies of mulberry trees, four solid buildings, and a cemetery remain of the quaint agricultural ghost town of Grafton.

Grafton was established by Mormon farmers on the south side of the Virgin River in 1859, part of the colonization process the Mormon Church undertook in Southern Utah (which they called *Dixie*) in the mid- and late-1800s. The Virgin is unpredictable, and in 1862 it rose against the settlers, washing away their town. So they relocated to higher ground, set out fruit orchards, planted corn and wheat, raised sheep, dabbled in cotton, and grew mulberry trees for the production of silk. Prosperity never arrived, however, and because of disease and Native American incursions, the town was abandoned for a short time between 1866 and 1868.

The peak population of Grafton appears to have been less than 200, and by 1920 only three families remained. The site has been used for the filming of several movies, including parts of *Butch Cassidy and the Sundance Kid*.

A plaque at the local cemetery sums up an incomplete but poignant picture of the hardships endured by these early pioneers:

"But when the year 1866 hit, the settlers must have wondered if their Heavenly Father had abandoned them. Thirteen people died in rapid succession, taken by epidemics, a tragic accident and by the friction caused when new folks rub up against old."

Such is the heritage of Grafton.

Located on a raised area a half-mile south of the town site, Grafton's cemetery holds graves dated from 1862 to 1924. Many are unmarked, but others tell stories of hardship, death, and much grieving among these sturdy pioneers trying to eek out a home in the wilderness, truly strangers in an unfriendly land. The York family lost three young children to diphtheria in seven days. The Field family lost a mom and two daughters within a couple of days. Two families each lost a young teenager when a swing broke, killing them in the fall. Surrounded by a wooden fence are the graves of Joseph, Robert, and Mary Berry, killed April 2, 1866, in a nearby American Indian attack. And so the stories roll.

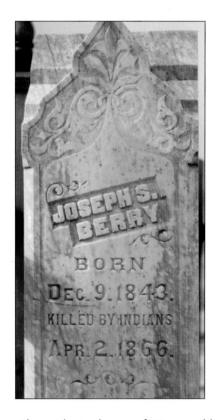

Above: The tombstone of 22-year-old Joseph S. Berry tells a tale of terror and violence once faced by one of Grafton's pioneering families.

Above: Grafton's adobe-brick multipurpose school/church/community center was built in 1886, and its last class ended in 1919 when only nine students remained. The building also hosted Friday night dances, drawing many folks from outlying farms and communities. To the right of the school is blacksmith Alonzo Russell's two-story adobe home, built in 1862. When Alonzo died in 1910, his son Frank moved in, remaining until 1944. He was Grafton's last resident when he moved out. Both buildings have been restored since this photo was taken in the mid-1990s. *Right:* In 1877, John and Ellen Wood built a cozy brick home on their small farm located just south of the center of town. They also built this log barn and smaller granary. Like the other buildings in Grafton, all the structures on the Wood property, as well as the split-rail fence, have been stabilized and restored.

The Tintic, Utah

Silver, silver, silver. That's what the Tintic Mining District was all about, more than $50 million in silver. The name came from Ute Chief Tintic.

This historic silver mining district straddles U.S. Highway 6, about 25 miles west of Interstate 15 at Santaquin. Today, the Tintic is a collection of forgotten names such as Dividend, Homansville, and Knightsville; rubbled sites such as Silver City; sleepy places such as Mammoth; and the area's metropolis: Eureka, with its 766 people (as of the 2000 census) and a *very* ghostly air.

Eureka's long main street is lined with mostly unoccupied buildings, all of which harken back to when it was *the* boom town of the Tintic. Silver was discovered here in December 1869; after subsequent discoveries, the true value of the deposits was real-

ized, and Eureka quickly placed itself at the leading edge of the district. Fire ravaged Eureka in 1893, but the town quickly rebuilt with one- and two-story brick and stone buildings, most of which remain intact today.

In 1910, Eureka had a population of 3,400 as well as the second J. C. Penney store in the country. In 1930, Eureka still had 3,041 folks, and it wasn't until 1942, when the mines were closed by Order L-208, that Eureka's population declined radically.

South of Eureka is the old town of Mammoth, where a fire station, cabins, and lots of rubble remain. The mine sits above the town on the side of a hill. In 1930, 750 people still lived in Mammoth, but only a few are there now.

Above left: On April 21, 1906, teachers from Juab and Eureka gathered for a convention at the four-year-old Church of Jesus Christ of Latter Day Saints meeting house. It was one of several churches in Eureka, and its Gothic Revival style stands out among the others. *Above:* Sitting in a draw midway up the north side of Eureka Ridge, south of Eureka itself, the Centennial-Eureka Mine was one of the largest mines in the Tintic Mining District. This image dates to around 1900 when the mine employed about 100 workers. It closed in 1927 after producing around 45,000 ounces of gold and 21 million ounces of silver.

Above left: Dead buildings, boarded-up windows, faded advertisements, peeling paint, cracked concrete sidewalks, and crumbling storefronts mark Eureka's Main Street today. The historic value of this now-quiet town and surrounding mining district was recognized in 1979 when Eureka and the Tintic Mining District were listed with the National Register of Historic Places.
Above: Located high above Mammoth on the east side, the Mammoth Shaft looks out over the old mining town. Mammoth's mines were discovered in 1870, and the town has experienced several ups and downs, with its peak years being 1900–1910. *Left:* Dating to 1869, Silver City reached a population of 800, a number which faded after a 1902 fire. In 1907 the huge Knight Mill was built, and a second boom enveloped Silver City. More than 100 new buildings were built, and some 1,500 folks called Silver City home, at least until 1915, when the mill closed and Silver City died for good.

Topaz, Utah

Shortly after the fateful morning of December 7, 1941, when the Japanese Navy attacked Pearl Harbor, the United States of America was swept up in a wave of anti-Japanese hysteria. It didn't take long into 1942 before ten relocation centers scattered about the American West were hastily banged together to hold Japanese Americans.

Consisting of 623 buildings, Topaz Relocation Center was built in the western Utah desert about 16 miles northwest of Delta. Opening on September 11, 1942, it became the new home for more than 8,000 detainees, which made it Utah's fifth largest city. The entire complex covered 19,800 acres, but the main portion was a square-mile core of buildings in 42 numbered blocks. Of these blocks, 34 contained look-alike clusters, each with 12 barracks and an administrative building on either side of a central mess hall, latrine, and laundry. Six other blocks contained sports fields, a gymnasium, churches, schools, and other common-use facilities.

Along the north side of the site were military police quarters, the hospital, administrative offices, staff housing, and warehouses. All of this was surrounded by barbed-wire fencing and secured by armed MPs sitting atop a half-dozen 50-foot guard towers. The other 30 square miles of land were used for agricultural purposes for the self-sufficient camp.

When World War II ended, these camps were no longer needed, so on October 31, 1945, Topaz was closed. The buildings were removed shortly thereafter.

As a plaque at the entrance of the main site reads: "The memory of Topaz remains a tribute to a people whose faith and loyalty was steadfast—while America's had faltered."

Above: Block 7 and part of Block 6 of Topaz Relocation Center can be seen in a view looking toward the northwest. The buildings with white ends in the background are part of the hospital, as is the boiler house smokestack in the upper right corner. In the barracks blocks, the mess hall and latrine buildings run at right angles to the barracks themselves.
Left: This watercolor birthday card was painted by an internee. The Kanji script reads, "Happy Birthday, April 2x 1945, Miss Gerard." (The second number of the date has been cut off.)

World War II Relocation Centers

WHEN THE EMPIRE of Japan attacked Pearl Harbor, it set off a tsunami of Japanophobia across the United States. In response to an intense and unfounded fear that Japanese Americans could and would collaborate with the enemy, on February 19, 1942, President Franklin Roosevelt issued Executive Order 9066, which was followed on March 18 by Executive Order 9102. Together, these two orders opened the door to the removal of more than 120,000 American citizens of Japanese descent. They were forced to sell everything they owned and relocate to 17 temporary assembly centers, from which they were farmed out to ten hastily built relocation centers, located in America's hinterlands, far from the heavily populated coastal and military-industrial complex areas.

The 15 temporary assembly centers were located at Mayer and Parker Dam, Arizona; Portland, Oregon; and Puyallup, Washington; as well as a dozen California locations at Fresno, Manzanar, Marysville, Merced, Pinedale, Pomona, Sacramento, Salinas, Santa Anita, Stockton, Tanforan, Tulare, and Turlock. The ten relocation centers were located at Gila River and Poston, Arizona; Jerome and Rohwer, Arkansas; Manzanar and Tule Lake, California; Granada, Colorado; Minidoka, Idaho; Topaz, Utah; and Heart Mountain, Wyoming. There were additional, smaller Department of Justice, U.S. Army, and other War Relocation Authority facilities.

Top: This photograph circa 1942 shows relocated Japanese American internees unloading their belongings and moving into the barracks at the Central Utah Relocation Center, later renamed Topaz Relocation Center. Most of the detainees at this camp were from the San Francisco Bay area. *Above:* Concrete slabs and walls remain of the hospital's boiler house and are the largest of the ruins left at this site. The boiler was coal-fired and provided hot water for the hospital. The coal was mined by miners from the camp at the Dog Valley Mine, located south of present-day Interstate 70, south of Emery, about 80 air-miles southeast of Delta.

Animas Forks, Colorado

Sitting at an elevation of 11,184 feet in the mine-studded Animas River Valley in the heart of the San Juan Mountains of southwestern Colorado, Animas Forks is one of the highest ghost towns in the country. Weather-beaten, chocolate-brown, wooden buildings hearken back to the days when the Silverton Northern Railway threaded its way 12 miles up the canyon from Silverton, gold and silver flowed back down toward that town, and 450 people called this valley home—at least in the summer—until the 1890s, when it began to fade.

Still standing is the famous two-story William Duncan House, with its magnificent bay windows, that unfounded local legend says was once owned by Tom Walsh, the owner of the nearby Camp Bird Mine above Ouray. He sold his mine holdings in 1902 to become a multimillionaire, and the family moved to Washington, D.C., where he built the famous Walsh-McLean House (which is now the Indonesian Embassy). His daughter, Evalyn Walsh, married publishing heir Edward "Ned" Beale McLean in 1908. In 1932, she inherited her parents' estate, including the mansion, when her mother died. Four years later, she wrote her memoirs, *Father Struck It Rich*. Rumor had it that she lived in the Animas Forks house while writing it.

Evalyn Walsh McLean was wealthy and eccentric. She was also a socialite who, from 1911 until 1947, was the last private owner of the magnificent, deep blue, 45.52 carat Hope Diamond and its associated curse.

Top: Looking almost like a watercolor painting, the Frisco-Bagley Mine, its 150-ton electrical-powered reduction mill, and the mine manager's house decorate the slope above the West Fork of the Animas River, a half mile west of Animas Forks. In 1912, the mill's prefabricated pieces were hauled by train to Animas Forks and then by wagon to the mine owned by the Bagley-Frisco Mines and Tunnel Company. The building, assembled around the preplaced machinery, remained in operation until the late 1920s. During World War II, the metallic components were sent out for scrap. The building itself was stabilized in 1990, and in May 2005 it was placed on the Colorado State Register of Historic Properties. *Above:* In this photograph circa 1878, Animas Forks was a small town of 30 homes and 250 people, a general store, a post office, and a saloon. By 1885 it had doubled in population to 450 people, and its businesses consisted of two assay offices, a boarding house, a hotel, and several saloons and stores.

BOOM AND BUST

The Silverton-Northern Railway reached Animas Forks in 1904, breathing life into what was then a fading town, being kept alive by the Gold Prince and Frisco-Bagley Mine. In 1910, the Gold Prince closed when its operations were shifted to Eureka. The year after that, the Frisco-Bagley Mine was extended 7,500 feet into the mountains, and its 32 miners and 10 mill workers kept Animas Forks breathing, albeit in a labored manner. The post office finally closed in 1915, and by the end of the 1920s, Animas Forks was a ghost town. More recently, the scattered remnants of Animas Forks, such as the two-story William Duncan House built in 1879 (*at left and below in left bottom corner*), have been stabilized by the Bureau of Land Management. That was made possible by the solid construction of most of these buildings, which was necessary because of the heavy snow and long, brutal winters.

Nevadaville, Colorado

Poor Nevadaville, sitting forgotten like a castoff light bulb. Located a mile southwest of Central City and Black Hawk, two neon-lit Rocky Mountain gambling havens, it was a key player in establishing "The Richest Square Mile on Earth." Unlike those other two towns, however, Nevadaville is quiet, sprinkled with red-brick buildings lining a dirt main street. Its ghost town aura virtually glows.

Established 1859 as Nevada City, it had 2,705 people in 1860 but was wiped off the map by a fast-moving fire in 1861. The town bounced back, bigger and better, officially as Bald Mountain—its unpopular post office name. Nevada City/Bald Mountain peaked in the 1860s when the town blended into Central City, which in turn became part of Black Hawk, all amalgamated and mixed together like modern, faceless suburbia.

In 1868, however, there came a big compromise in which the town officially became Nevadaville. (The post office, however, remained Bald Mountain until it closed in 1921.) That wasn't enough to sustain the town, however, and Nevadaville's radiance dimmed until only two residents remained in 1930.

Today, six people watch over the town's handful of remaining ruins, homes, and commercial buildings, which include a combination city hall/firehouse; a couple of stores; a saloon; and the renovated, two-story brick Masonic Lodge built in 1879 for a cost of $7,471.35. That majestic relic currently houses Nevada Lodge #4 of the Ancient Free and Accepted Masons of Colorado. In 1965, after more than 20 years of dormancy, the lodge hosted its first "Ghost Town Meeting." It was a hit. The lodge meets monthly, except in winter!

This view of Nevadaville looks northeast across the west end of the town. The large buildings in the foreground house the Gold Coin Mines Company Mine and Mill, and mine-studded Nevada Hill rises directly behind town in the background. Downtown Nevadaville is on the far right. The town's two churches lie just above the peak of the tall portion of the largest mill building. Even though Nevadaville peaked in the 1860s, it was still home to more than 1,000 people in 1900. Today, however, after multiple fires and the march of time, most of the buildings visible in this photo are no longer in existence.

Above: On the south side of Main Street, the wood-frame City Hall building housed city offices on the top floor, a fire department on the first floor, and a two-cell, metal-walled jail in the basement. It's the only wooden commercial building to survive Nevadaville's numerous fires. *Above right:* Rock wall ruins are all that are left of an old store building basement on the south side of Main Street.
Right: The two-story, brick Masonic Hall was built in 1879 to replace a building the Masons were leasing. The lodge's membership followed the town's population, and by the 1940s, the remaining members of Lodge #4 met in Central City. Lodge meetings in the 1950s featured debates on whether to sell, renovate, or tear down this building. Thankfully for ghost-town aficionados today, renovation prevailed, and in 1965, fund-raisers were held to begin the process. In the 1970s, restoration began, and today Lodge #4 has returned home. The smaller three-arched building to the right of the hall is a former saloon.

St. Elmo, Colorado

The town of St. Elmo had it all. Established around 1880 as Forest City, this booming gold town, stagecoach hub, and railroad construction camp had 400 or so people. The narrow-gauge Denver, South Park, and Pacific Railroad was punching its 1,845-foot-long Alpine Tunnel through the mountains west of St. Elmo while the mines released their treasure.

But the U.S. Post Office didn't like the name Forest City. Three people got together to brainstorm. Someone remembered a popular novel by Augusta Jane Evans called *St. Elmo*, and everyone agreed. Forest City was renamed St. Elmo.

Through the 1880s, St. Elmo bustled, with as many as 2,000 residents. That all changed in 1890 when fire swept through. The storekeeper/postmaster was the hero of the day, saving the mail. He couldn't save his store, however, and lost the town's cigar and liquor supply. In all, two blocks of businesses were incinerated and not rebuilt.

People moved on after that, and in 1910, the Alpine Tunnel closed, leaving St. Elmo as the end of the line. The Mary Murphy Mine kept 100 employed until 1922, when it shut down after producing 220,000 ounces of gold. Four years later, the train stopped running altogether.

Three people remain today, and St. Elmo looks like a ghost town should. Its 40 or so worn, wooden buildings turn empty faces onto a dirt main street in the forested Chalk River Valley uphill from Nathrop.

This view looks north across the west end of Main Street from Hancock Road—which followed the Denver, South Park, and Pacific Railroad line uphill towards Romley. The large building in the center is the Stark Brothers store, the post office, and Home Comfort Hotel. The building in the right corner is the American House Hotel. During its heyday in the 1880s, St. Elmo filled this forested bowl with numerous businesses, including general stores, five hotels, saloons, dance halls, a telegraph office, a newspaper, a post office, a school, and the town hall. Unfortunately, the town has suffered several fires, including one in 2002. Today St. Elmo is listed on the National Register of Historic Places.

STANDING IN SILENCE

On April 15, 2002, an electrical fire destroyed the St. Elmo Town Hall and jail, a mule barn, the Stark family residence, and two other buildings. The Town Hall (*at left*) was one of the town's original buildings that had been spared by previous fires. After this most recent blaze, the Town Hall property was donated to the Buena Vista Heritage Museum. Unlike the other structures, which are now memories and vacant lots, it has been rebuilt. But the once-bustling Main Street of St. Elmo is quiet now. Visitors no longer venture in and out of Stark's Home Comfort Hotel, nor do the doors to the Stark Brothers' Store and post office open and close with the passing of shoppers. The Starks were the last of the old-time families in St. Elmo, with the final family member leaving in 1958, six years after the post office closed.

Silverton, Colorado

Wicked, wicked Blair Street. The city elders couldn't (or wouldn't) shut it down, and the $500 annual fees payable by dance halls and saloons, plus the $5 monthly fines against the "ladies," barely dented the raucousness. Vigilante justice, drunken brawls, knifings, shootings, and claim-jumping were all in a day's work for officers of the law.

Sitting in the heart of Southwestern Colorado's San Juan Mountains, Silverton was the ultimate boomtown, the Silver Queen of Colorado. Gold and silver were found by the ton in the mountains surrounding the 9,300-foot high mountain bowl along the Animas River.

Beginning in 1874, miners flocked here in droves, followed by other camp hangers-on. The town site was laid out, and within a few months the population passed the 500 mark. In 1882, the railroad arrived, and the real boom began. The town turned into a city, and the population arched upward toward 3,000. Blocks of substantial buildings were erected and remain today. Fraternal lodges, churches, a library, a courthouse, and other amenities tamed the wild edge—a bit.

Silverton stumbled a little in the 1893 Silver Panic, but the first half of the 20th century was brutal to the Silver Queen. In October 1918, a flu epidemic killed 146 people. Silver lost 50 percent of its value in 1920, shuttering mines. That trend continued through 1942, when Order L-208 took care of the rest. After World War II, the new gold came from tourism, which staved off Silverton's encroaching ghostdom.

Above: This view looks south over Silverton toward Sultan Mountain circa 1901. At the beginning of the boom in the early 1880s, Silverton consisted of 300–400 homes, 50–75 businesses, several hotels, and the appropriate city and county govern-ment buildings. *Left:* By 1940, the date of this photo, the Silver Lake Mill, a massive, low-grade silver mining complex near Silverton, was starting to show the effects of aging and neglect. Active from 1890 to 1900, the mill burned in 1907 and was rebuilt. In its lifetime, it processed more than 500,000 tons of low-grade ore worth more than $7 million. The Silverton Northern Railroad ran a branch line to the complex from town.

Construction began on the San Juan County courthouse in August 1906, and 16 months later it was open for business. San Juan County is the least populated of Colorado's counties, and only three of the 64 counties in the state are smaller in area. Silverton is the county's only living town, so the county population mirrors Silverton's. The majestic brick courthouse has been modernized—it's an interesting juxtaposition to see state-of-the-art computers in a century-old building.

Population Figures for Silverton

Year	Population
1875 (est.)	100
1876 (est.)	500
1883 (est.)	3,000
1899 (est.)	2,000
1918 (est.)	1,500
1930 (census)	1,301
1950 (census)	1,375
1960 (census)	822
1970 (census)	797
1980 (census)	794
1990 (census)	716
2000 (census)	531
2005 (est.)	548

The San Juan County Courthouse dome peeks above the last building on the right in this photo looking north along the west side of Greene Street. From left to right, all but one of these historic buildings date to Silverton's glory days. From left are: two structures that are each called the Lacy Building—the orange, from 1883, and the purple, from 1884, which once housed the Senate Saloon; the 1983 light blue, two-story building (which replaced a building torn down in the late 1970s); the 1890 two-tone, single-story Malchus Building; and the 1876 white Silverton Standard Building. The latter is the oldest commercial building still in use in the town. The large, light blue, brick edifice next to it is the 1880 Posey Wingate building, Silverton's first large brick structure. Beyond are the 1895 Bausman Building, the Cole Hoffman Building, and the 1902 Wyman Building.

Southeast Colorado Farm Towns

The dry, pancake-flat grasslands on the "other side" of Colorado (the southeastern corner) have given rise to a crop of small agricultural and railroad supported towns, many of which are long dead or are fading into ghost-town status. These forgotten ghosts, gaunt skeletons of tiny towns, don't get much attention, and as a result, their stories seldom see print, unlike their more boisterous mountain-based mining town cousins. But each location had its promise and its cluster of settlers. Each person staking their future here was filled with hopes and dreams of success.

As those hopes and dreams dried up, the towns faded. Railroad stations ceased operation. With declining populations, post offices closed. Stores, gas stations, and schools with no customers or students shut down in town after town after town.

The few remaining communities showing any semblance of life lie along state highways, but most have few or no traveler amenities. As time marches on, the towns die off. Names such as Model, Tyrone, Thatcher, Timpas, Arlington, Haswell, Chivington, Brandon, and Sheridan Lake barely even qualify as dots on the map—forgotten by all but a few.

What does the tiny jail in Haswell have left to say? Who was held there? Where did the waitress from the Sheridan Lake Café move? What happened to the last class at the Timpas School? These questions will probably never be answered as the mists of time are closing in on these dying little towns.

Built in Brandon to view the total solar eclipse of June 8, 1918, this 60-foot telescope tower was much larger than the town's school building. On the left side of the schoolhouse was equipment set up to record the eclipse. When the eclipse reached Brandon in the late afternoon, the period of totality was just shy of one and a half minutes.

Left: In 1916, Timpas, Colorado, was full of promise and expectations, both of which have dried up and blown away in the ever-present wind. Today, the Timpas School is a hollow shell filled with memories. *Below:* Brandon's desiccated main street still runs past dead businesses such as this old false front. The town once had a bank, a general store, a gas station, and a post office (1888–1963), as well as a few other businesses.

Top left: In 2000, only 66 people lived in Sheridan Lake. This beautiful old school building, which once echoed to the excited shouts of kids playing, is quieter these days. It currently serves as the faded town's post office. *Above:* In 2008, the Census Bureau estimated Haswell's population at 70. The streets are spotted with vacant buildings such as this old store, a gas station, and the tiny 12-foot by 14-foot jail. The still-active post office was established in 1903. In 1920, Haswell incorporated, and ten years later it had 156 folks. They were served by numerous businesses, including two general stores, a hardware store, a bank, a hotel, a restaurant, a post office, a school, a church, a newspaper, a barber, a pool hall, a meat market, a blacksmith, a livery stable, a harness shop, and a lumberyard. That was all undermined by the Depression and the Dust Bowl. *Left:* Delhi's "One Stop" Store once provided all the food, gasoline, and automotive repair needs of this agricultural town established along the railroad in 1892. A post office operated here between the years of 1908 and 1913 and again between 1919 and 1975.

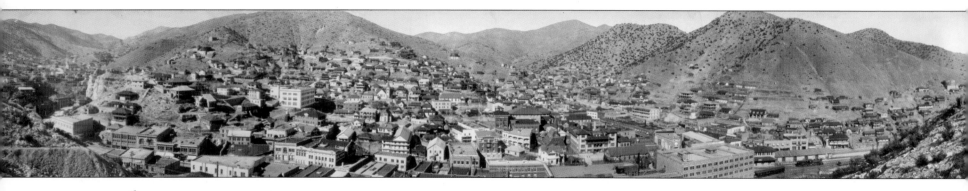

Bisbee, Arizona

Boom and bust, copper and rust, Bisbee and its colorful assortment of 6,000 people does not meet normally accepted connotations of what a ghost town is. But behind that first impression is the truth. Bisbee has waned. Its zenith was in the early 1900s when it had around 20,000 residents.

The dry Arizona desert puckers up into mineral-rich mountains in numerous places. Just 20 miles south of Tombstone and seven miles north of the Mexico-U.S. border, the Mule Mountains are one of those puckers.

Sprawling up the arms of a V-shape gulch on the south side of the Mule Mountains is the majestic old copper-mining city of Bisbee. The Queen Mine lies below, a massive hole in the earth that yielded eight *billion* pounds of copper, as well as millions of ounces of gold and silver and millions of pounds of lead, zinc, and other minerals. This mine made Bisbee the undisputed "Queen of the Copper Camps" and put it on the map, keeping it there for more than 100 years.

Today's Bisbee is a funky, fun town filled with free spirits, frivolity, and festivals, all playing up the good old days. Bisbee's charm lies in the fact that a major fire completely wiped out the rambling tinderbox town in 1908. By 1910, however, the ashes were replaced by what is there now, a living museum filled with 1910 architecture.

After Bisbee burned on October 14, 1908, it came back. Not as a singed and wounded little mining camp, but as a bustling, solid city and one of the largest mining towns in the country. This 1916 view looks east across Tombstone Canyon toward Chihuahua Hill.

Chihuahua Hill rises to the east of present-day Bisbee, marking the site with its famous B. Bisbee's streets are quiet now, but it still maintains its importance as the Cochise County seat, an honor it wrested from Tombstone, the alleged "Town Too Tough to Die," in 1929. Fires, floods, and the up-and-down uncertainties of the mining business have not killed this survivor—they may have dimmed the lights, but they didn't extinguish them.

Top left: The Lavender Pit, viewed here from the north, was Bisbee's true "Money Pit" until December 1974. This money pit didn't absorb money, however; it produced massive quantities of it. *Left:* Phelps Dodge Mining Company opened the Copper Queen Hotel in 1902. It was built to house important visitors, giving them a comfortable and classy place to stay. Continuing to do business today, the 52-room Copper Queen is Arizona's oldest still-operational hotel. *Above:* Other than paint and details such as asphalt paving and modern cars, downtown Bisbee hasn't changed much since its 1910 rebuild. *Top:* From 1932 until 1934, Arizona's license plates were solid copper, extolling its copper mining heritage. Unfortunately, due to copper's inherent softness and the state's rough roads, many of the copper license plates suffered metal fatigue around the bolt holes, causing them to tear and allowing the heavy plates to fall off vehicles. In 1935, Arizona reverted to copper-colored steel license plates. Problem solved!

Goldroad and Oatman, Arizona

It took tough people to make a go of it in the hostile desert country of 19th-century Arizona. Maybe that's why it took so long for miners to penetrate the harsh terrain of northwestern Arizona's Black Mountains. In 1900, Jose Jerez discovered gold west of Sitgreaves Pass, and in 1902, Ben Paddock (some sources say Taddock) found gold at the Elephant's Tooth, a monolith at today's Oatman. Both discoverers sold out to organized mining companies that quickly moved in.

Ka-ching! At Goldroad, the little gold camp played sweet music off and on, ran a population of several hundred, and finally shut down in 1942. In 1949 the buildings were semidismantled so the owner wouldn't have to pay property taxes on usable but empty buildings.

Oatman's story differs, however. The Vivian post office opened in 1904 then changed names to Oatman in 1909. Oatman's mines were richer, and the location was better than Goldroad. Wild, younger brother Oatman quickly outgrew and outperformed its civic sibling. Some 10,000 people flocked here, but they left just as quickly when the Tom Reed Mine shut down in the 1930s. That left Oatman's remaining folks to cater to travelers along Route 66, which lasted until the 1950s, when the road was realigned, isolating Oatman and its 60 residents.

The quirky former mining town was rediscovered in the 1960s by tourists who still come by the busload to see the "Real West." They're met by Main Street's four-legged, long-eared greeters, burros with fast ice cream–sucking lips!

Picturesque ruins along the highway and tucked up and down washes leading off old Route 66 for about a mile and a half are all that remain of Goldroad. Despite off-and-on mining activity, the town has remained dead.

The Goldroad Mine kept the town of Goldroad alive until the operation closed in 1942. New owners reopened the mine in 1995, producing gold until 1998, when it shut down again. Tours of the underground workings were offered until 2007.

Above left: This old sign hangs out over the front of the historic, two-story, adobe-walled Oatman Hotel, which began life in 1902 as the Drulin Hotel. It offered miners and travelers eight rooms and was refurbished in the 1920s. In March 1939, movie stars Clark Gable and Carole Lombard gave the old hotel a tourism boost by spending their wedding night there. Once mining ended, Route 66 travelers needing a place to spend the night kept the old hotel open. In the 1960s it was renamed the Oatman Hotel, but today it no longer rents out rooms, as it has been turned into a museum. The restaurant, however, still serves meals. The hotel is said to be haunted, with claims of three different ghosts roaming the halls and rooms. *Above:* The 300-seat former Oatman Theatre Building stopped showing movies by 1945. Today it houses a retail store, and its shady porch provides a great place to sit and watch life, and the ubiquitous burros, march up and down the street. *Left:* The Oatman Mercantile and Lee Lumber Company building is one of many ancient, weathered, and repainted storefronts along Main Street catering to the 500,000 tourists who flock annually to see a tiny part of the Old West and Route 66. Residents of Oatman hang out the bunting and invite them in with open arms.

Superior, Arizona

Imagine driving down a modern highway past modern road-town amenities such as busy gas stations, mini-marts, and video rental shops on a warm Saturday afternoon. Suddenly the vehicle is yanked off the highway and deposited in the middle of a four-way intersection, in the middle of a dead downtown. Empty storefronts stretch in every direction—no cars, no people. Nothing but empty storefronts.

This is not *The Twilight Zone*. This is real life. Welcome to Superior, Arizona.

Like Bisbee, Arizona; Silverton, Colorado; and Galena, Illinois, Superior is a living town, a by-product from the flush days of when it was a booming copper mining outpost. Similar to Bisbee and Galena, it still has a large resident population. But Superior has a unique twist: The main business district is dead—not just a few scattered buildings, but a solidly lined, dead main street.

Superior has seen little print in ghost-town literature, but it is a true gem dating to 1910 when the Magma Copper Mining Company purchased the former Silver King mine and support town of Superior (renamed from Hastings in 1900). Magma went for the copper and found it. With more than 4,000 people during the Great Depression, Superior was one of the few bright economic spots in a depressed economy.

But its prosperity is fading. In 1970, the census recorded 5,028 folks, but the July 2007 Census Bureau estimate was down to 3,001. Superior's copper mines are now quiet. The dead downtown beckons. The ghosts are encroaching.

Above: The tall, brick smokestack at the former Magma Copper Mining Company smelter complex west of town announces Superior from a distance. This standing reminder points to the day when Superior truly lived up to its name. The site is currently owned by the Resolution Copper Mining Company. *Left:* Perched at the far eastern end of Main Street, the La Mina Bar on the left side of the block is one of a few businesses still operating in downtown Superior. Just to its right, Griffen's Market runs a perpetual "SALE" in a vacant building.

Above: Scattered throughout many of Arizona's dead and dying mining towns are the bright red-and-white shells of Sprouse Reitz Company's five & dime stores. In the 1960s, the company had grown to more than 400 stores, mostly in urban areas. Many, however, were sited in early to mid–20th-century mining towns. The company closed its last store in 1993, but these brightly colored vacant shells remain, greeting ghost-town visitors. *Above right:* This vintage postcard features a view of the town around 1915.

Above: Standing guard over the upper end of town, Superior High School, built in 1926, no longer echoes to the sounds of education. The last graduating class walked out the doors around 2002.

The classic, single-screened Uptown Theater, with a balcony and seating for 850, once served as Superior's premium entertainment venue. Built in 1923, the "Art Moderne" theater was demolished in 2008.

Vulture Mine, Arizona

Henry Wickenburg was a real character. How did he come to find and name the rich gold ledge that evolved into the Vulture Mine? The year was 1863 and . . .

Wickenburg was out prospecting and saw a group of buzzards soaring around what is now Vulture Peak.

Or he was out prospecting and shot a vulture. When he picked it up, he saw a number of gold nuggets lying around where the bird fell.

Or, in what may be everyone's favorite gold-find story, vultures were circling overhead as Wickenburg chased his runaway burro, chucking rocks at it. Of course, the rocks contained gold.

Or, how about Wickenburg's personal version? Henry and a partner were prospecting, but his partner fell ill and remained back at camp while Henry continued looking. Getting frustrated, he sat down to rest. And the rocks he rested against were laced with rich gold ore.

One of those stories, or something like it, is the truth. Wickenburg established his mine and then leased it out. In 1866, he sold an 80-percent interest in it to some New Yorkers—he only received the $20,000 down payment out of the total $85,000 promised, however. Even after litigation, he never got the balance, nor any returns on his one-fifth share. Bitter and broken, Wickenburg retired to his ranch outside the nearby town of Wickenburg, where in 1905 he shot himself in the head, ending his long, often painful, life.

The Vulture Mine possibly produced as much as $20 million in gold. Today it's a privately owned site where tourists can take their own self-guided tours through the authentic, unrestored mining camp.

Above: A rickety headframe stands over the inclined western shaft of the Vulture Mine, which supported a busy little mining camp containing hundreds of residents during several boom periods. *Below:* The Central Arizona Mining Company's office building, shown here in 1978, included the company's general office, an assay laboratory, a gold storage vault, and sleeping rooms for company officials. It was built in the 1880s using gold-bearing rock from the mine.

Above left: This crumbling adobe is said to have been a hotel, but legend maintains that the "hotel" housed single ladies rather than travelers. It opened in the 1870s and closed in 1942, when the entire camp shut down for the duration of World War II. The adobe-walled section with the collapsing roof was built in the 1870s and is the oldest part of the building. The newer section on the left was built in the 1880s, using the same gold-bearing rock from the mine as the office building. *Above:* The second of two schools was built in 1936 to serve the greater number of children in the camp during the 1930s. It also closed in 1942. *Far left:* This is an interior view of the assay office laboratory as it appeared in 1942. *Near left:* As can be seen here, the sleeping rooms in the mining company building weren't much better.

Chloride is filled with many different buildings of various designs and materials. This steep-roofed rock home was built in 1921 by longtime resident Austin Crawford. The roof's steep pitch was intended to deflect the large hailstones which he believed God would rain down. He included no inside doors, and each room was designed to be entered only from the outside. A later resident, artist and furniture builder Cassie Hobbs, used the building as a workshop, calling it her "Doodle-Dum." In July 1997, the house was added to New Mexico Historic Preservation Division's State Register of Cultural Properties.

Chloride, New Mexico

English teamster Harry Pye's claim to fame was that he found a rich silver lead in 1879 and was subsequently killed by Apache a few months later while working his claims. His legacy: Chloride, New Mexico.

Chloride was established in 1880, its tents filling the canyon bottom along Chloride Creek at the mouth of Chloride Creek Canyon in the Black Range mountains northwest of Truth or Consequences. In 1881, a real townsite was laid out, and seven businesses and 20 houses were built. Chloride boomed through the 1880s and began to decline after the silver market crashed in 1893. Even though Chloride faded, however, it was never totally abandoned. As a result, a number of old buildings remain along with 11 or so residents.

In 1977, the fate of Chloride was changed by a retired couple. Don and Dona Edmund were touring the back roads of New Mexico looking for unique and interesting places to visit and possibly settle. Upon arriving in Chloride, they knew this was to be their new home. They purchased a house and settled down amidst the handful of remaining old-timers, the last of whom passed away in 1999. Over time the Edmunds purchased more property and buildings, restoring many, including the 1880 Pioneer Store building built by James Dalglish. That location is now operated as the Pioneer Store Museum.

In *New Mexico's Best Ghost Towns,* author Philip Varney sums up this wonderful little semi-ghost best: "It's what you hope for from a ghost town but so seldom find."

Right: Located nine miles west of Chloride, the Silver Monument Mine was the largest and most productive of the mines that supported the town. Through 1926, it produced $680,000 in silver. This photo, circa 1906, shows from left to right: Mrs. Charley Hullinger, Larry Hartshorn, "Pap" Ed Davisson, Eddie Schmidt (*seated*), Mr. Bouton, Charley Hullinger, Raymond Schmidt, and Amy Schmidt.

Of the 30 or so remaining buildings in Chloride, these two are the best known. The restored Monte Cristo saloon graces the left, and the Pioneer Store Museum is on the right. Both are listed on the State Register of Cultural Properties.

Gunfighters of the Old West

Two MEN STOOD motionless in the rutted, dirt street at high noon, the only movement coming from a slight breeze stirring small swirls of street dust. Steely glares, hands poised for a draw, the men faced each other just a few yards apart. A grievance needed righting. Someone had to pay.

Bam! Bam! Twin puffs of smoke issued from the business end of one pistol. One man fell, a pair of lead slugs freeing his spirit. The other turned, walked to his horse, hopped on, and rode off into the noonday heat, leaving another victim of his .45 caliber Colt Peacemaker lying in the dust.

So goes the legend in the raw, wild, lawless West.

Butch Cassidy, Wyatt Earp, John Wesley Hardin, Wild Bill Hickok, Doc Holliday, Jesse James, Billy the Kid, Bat Masterson, Luke Short, Ben Thompson. . . . Were these legendary gunfighters badge-wearing, heroic law officers? Or just quick-drawing, opportunistic thugs with twitchy trigger fingers, chips on their shoulders, and lives lived on the other side of societal law? Or were they something in between, flitting back and forth as circumstances required?

The gun smoke of these duelers created a demand for law and order, more than 30 years' worth of lively legends, and thousands of pockmarked walls and bullet-holed windows. Chloride, for its part, was relatively free of such trouble—was it because of the "Hangin' Tree" on the town's main thoroughfare? More than 100 years later, its hard to tell. But flourishing between the end of the Civil War and the turn of the 20th century, these gunfighters were real people who, like today's celebrities, got quite a bit of press. They also were good with the gun, living by it and often dying by it.

Shown above is the interior of the Pioneer Store Museum, which opened in 1998. James Dalglish originally built this store of ponderosa pine logs around 1880. In 1897, he leased it out when he moved to nearby Hillsboro, opening a store there. In 1908, he sold it to the U.S. Treasure Mining Company, which operated it as a company store until 1923. The Edmunds purchased it and all the fixtures and merchandise in 1989, restoring it to the original. Displays include original shelving, counters, furniture, tools, a safe, merchandise, and other items commonly found in late-19th-century general stores.

Left: Photographer Henry Schmidt photographed his own house in Lake Valley on July 4, 1897. Schmidt was a well-known assayer and photographer in the region, taking many pictures of the buildings and mines in the mining towns of Lake Valley, Chloride, Winston, and Tyrone. In 1905 he and his family moved to nearby Chloride. His Lake Valley house is now known as the Nowlin House. *Below:* Nineteen-year-old Blanche Wilson arrived in Lake Valley with her family in 1908. She eventually married the Santa Fe Railroad station agent, A. Lee Nowlin, and moved into the former Schmidt house, becoming the building's new namesake. They ran the Continental Oil Company service station until he died in 1937. She remained here until her death in 1982.

Lake Valley, New Mexico

Lake Valley, now a quiet, dusty, ghost town administered by the Bureau of Land Management, sits along a state highway northeast of Deming. A dozen or so buildings remain standing, some of them quite substantial.

Lake Valley's boom-bust cycles began with the discovery of rich silver ore by George Lufkin in August 1878. Other claims were staked, and development began. George Daly, a mining promoter, arrived and purchased all those claims.

Deep in one of these mines, a massive ore pocket of almost pure silver was discovered— silver crystals glittered in the light from miner's candles. Called the Bridal Chamber, its value surpassed $15,000 per ton. Needless to say, Lake Valley boomed, quickly sprawling into a rowdy mining town supporting more than a thousand residents.

Peace was maintained by Sheriff Timothy Isaiah "Longhair Jim" Courtright, the tough-as-nails former marshal of Fort Worth, Texas, five years before he ended up on the wrong end of gunfighter Luke Short's pistol.

In 1893, the national silver panic crippled mining, and Lake Valley quickly faded. A major fire in June 1895 decimated the town, leaving little for the couple hundred residents still there. What remained barely clung to life through the first half of the 20th century.

The railroad shut down in 1934. Some manganese was mined in the mid-1940s and 1950s, but the post office finally closed in 1954, along with the mine and the rest of town. Lake Valley's last residents hung in there until 1994, when the Bureau of Land Management arrived. That agency is currently in the process of preserving the remains of this fascinating mining town.

Above: Lake Valley Cemetery is the final resting place for many of Lake Valley's residents. It is located southeast of town on the south side of the state highway. Numerous headstones tell the tales of a tough life in a frontier mining town. *Right:* Hundreds of buildings once marked the raucous, brawling, silver-mining town of Lake Valley. Yesterday, the town sprawled across the New Mexico desert, but today, silence prevails. The bustling commercial district is gone, burned in 1895. The railroad is gone, the tracks pulled. The manganese miners are gone, the mines closed. Modern-day Lake Valley is a wonderful, colorful collection of old cabins, a few rock-walled buildings, ruins, and stillness.

Mogollón, New Mexico

In this wild mining town of 2,000 people, a reputed 14 saloons, and a pair of red-light districts, it seemed $20 million in gold and silver taken from the ground may have been secondary to liquor, women, gunplay, and robbery. Mogollón (pronounced mo-gee-YON) also seemed to suffer from a Sodom and Gomorrah complex, enduring the scourges of fire five times (in 1894, 1904, 1910, 1915, and 1942) and flood four times (in 1894, 1896, 1899, and 1914). Because of its isolation, this 20th-century mining town was steeped in 19th-century mining town morals. In fact, prohibition during the 1920s was pretty much ignored.

That might just sum up Mogollón, one of the state's best ghost towns. Despite being continuously burned out and washed out, as well as being ignored by the outside world—as long as its mineral wealth continued to flow— it boomed and busted several times en route to its final destiny in 1942 with Order L-208 and a final major fire.

What remain today are about 25 buildings and an equal number of people. Silver Creek still flows placidly down the north side of Main Street, a couple of museums try to ignite interest, and a pair of picturesque wooden false fronts at the east end of Main Street hold a little secret. They aren't what they appear!

The Blacksmith/General Store on the north side and the saloon across the street are not really the businesses they claim—they're Hollywood props, left over from the filming of a Henry Fonda movie, *My Name Is Nobody*.

Such is Mogollón: contradictory, yet fascinating.

Above: At the time of this Cinco de Mayo parade in 1914, Mogollón was at its peak, with some 2,000 people and a main street stretching half a mile lined with buildings. *Below:* A well-tended, still-occupied miner's cabin sits on the hillside overlooking Mogollón. Note the well and rock retaining wall.

Formerly called the Midway Theater, the Mogollón Theatre was built around the turn of the 20th century by Harry Herman, a local mill owner. Said to be the oldest intact theater building in New Mexico, it has been restored and is also used for special events.

Above: Downtown Mogollón is much smaller today than it was during the boom. To the left is the two-story, adobe J. P. Holland General Store, built in 1885. It started life as the Mogollón House, with a hotel upstairs and a general store below. James P. Holland bought it in 1914, operating his barbershop and general store and renting out the upstairs rooms to boarders. The business closed in 1948, and the building has since been renovated. It currently houses the Silver Creek Inn. The cluster of three buildings on the right includes a museum. *Left:* The Little Fannie Mine is on the site of the original silver/gold discovery in the 1870s, but it wasn't until the 1880s that any serious work occurred. This was one of Mogollón's largest mines, operating 24 hours a day until 1942. The corrugated sheet metal mill buildings were removed between the late 1970s and 2003.

Route 66 Ghosts in Texas

Route 66 was America's Main Street, the Mother Road, the westward route of the Okies during the Dust Bowl days. Stretching from Chicago to Santa Monica, California, it stitches together eight states. In Texas, Route 66 zipped across 178 miles of griddle-flat Panhandle stretching east and west of Amarillo. Only 9 percent of that pioneering route in Texas is lost; the rest is still drivable but has mostly been supplanted by Interstate 40. And in the Panhandle, ghosts of the old road towns remain, ripe for exploring.

With modern air-conditioned supercars cruising effortlessly down superwide superhighways, it's hard to imagine the difficulties encountered driving this route in its heyday from the 1930s to the '60s. Unlike today, drivers couldn't cruise for 300 or 400 miles without stopping. As a result, tiny towns popped up along the highway to serve the needs of travelers as well as to entertain them, protect them from the brutal heat and blowing dust in the summer, and keep them warm and cozy in the vicious cold of winter.

Today's forgotten map dots were yesterday's road towns. Glenrio, Alanreed, and a handful of other places provided comfort and service to travelers unsticking themselves from front seats and kids crawling stiffly out of back seats. Warm "eats," hot coffee, a tank of gas—"check under the hood?"—Minuteman service, and the U-Drop-Inn with its refrigerated air and free TV. All this was provided with a smile, all designed to make the traveler feel human again. This wasn't just America's Main Street. This *was* America.

THE CARS NO LONGER STOP

The desiccated road town of Glenrio is split by the New Mexico/Texas state line nearly dead center between the east and west anchors of Route 66. Depending on the direction of travel, it was either the first or last stop in Texas. Car "food" was provided at the Phillips 66 Station, people food at the Texas Longhorn Café, and a good night's rest at the motel. Glenrio's life began as a railroad siding in the early 1900s, and it thrived as a shipping center for farms and ranches. The town began capturing tourist traffic when the highway was built in the mid-1920s. Then came the Depression and the Dust Bowl days of the 1930s. After World War II, a rise in tourism brought increased traffic, which the 30 or so residents cared for and cultivated. Glenrio's reason to exist ended in 1973 when Interstate 40 diverted traffic off U.S. Highway 66.

Above: This 1951 Texas license plate is a relic of the glory years of the little road towns scattered across the top of Texas along Route 66. *Right:* The restored 1930s-era Bradley Kiser Super Service Gas Station was a popular way station in the tiny community of Alanreed. Today Alanreed barely clings to life as I-40 skirts along the north edge of town bringing some nostalgia-seeking tourists.

Left: Memories of Route 66's glory days abound in Alanreed, a nearly dead town that was once home to 500 residents. Here a forgotten café and gas station is sheltered by the shade of huge trees, a faded remnant of the "good old days." In the mid-20th century, Alanreed boasted of numerous tourist amenities, such as gas stations, repair garages, and cafés, all located between the oldest cemetery on the Texas portion of Route 66 and the 1904-era clapboard Baptist church on the west end of town. The town also played host to the Regal Reptile Ranch, a once-popular tourist attraction featuring live rattlesnakes and other reptilian critters that could be viewed—for a fee. Today, the captive rattlers are gone, as are most of the cross-country travelers. Alanreed's handful of still-active businesses continues to hang in there, trolling for tourists seeking to experience the aura of a once-bustling Route 66 road town.

Thurber, Texas

Only five people live in Thurber, Texas, once home to thousands, all living in an ultramodern company town with modern amenities of life such as full electrical power. Originally established in the mid-1880s midway between Fort Worth and Abilene in north-central Texas, this bituminous coal–mining town was electrified in 1895. Then in 1897, a brick kiln and brickyard were added, and paving bricks began to contribute to the economy.

At Thurber's mid-1910s peak, some 3,000 tons of coal a day poured from the Texas and Pacific Coal Company, union-operated underground mines dug by miners from nearly 20 nations. In 1917, oil was discovered nearby, and Thurber expanded to accommodate that industry. However, oil also contributed to the town's downfall, as the main market for coal was the railroads, which were converting locomotives over to oil burners, reducing the need for coal. Oil became popular and displaced coal, but the oil industry isn't as labor intensive and doesn't require the same numbers of workers.

In 1921, with coal production decreasing, the company proposed a devastating 33-percent wage reduction. The union countered with a 20-percent offer, which the company rejected. The mines were shut down, and a decade later, the brick kiln closed. Thurber's reason to exist was gone. By the end of the 1930s, the post office had closed, the last inhabitants had left, and most of the structures had been torn down. Thurber said good-bye.

Today, only mine-scarred hills, ruins, and half a dozen seen-better-days brick structures remain, including the famous 128-foot-tall smokestack, the old store (which is now a restaurant), and a museum.

Above: In 1895, Thurber was one of the earliest towns in Texas to be completely electrified. A dozen years later, the town, owned by the Texas and Pacific Coal Company, needed a larger power plant, so in 1908 a new plant was built of brick. Today, the smokestack and some low ruins are all that remain of Thurber's once-modern power plant. *Left:* Everybody in Thurber turned out for this flag-waving Fourth of July parade in the plaza likely sometime around the World War I era. Even the pig in the lower left corner seemed to be having a grand time participating in the festivities. Parades and holiday celebrations such as this were big social events in the days before the electronic diversions of radio and television, especially in hard-working communities such as Thurber. Workers and nonworkers alike had a chance to relax and socialize with each other.

Above: On Sunday, June 17, 1917, many in the town gathered on Thurber Square around the bandstand. The large brick building behind the people was a dry goods and furniture store. The white building on the right was a grocery store.

Left: One of Thurber's several bands was comprised of members of the United Mine Workers of America, Local Union 2763. Note the union's identification on the drum head, reflecting the fact that Thurber's mines were 100-percent unionized by 1903.
Above: Built in 1892, St. Barbara's Catholic Church was erected by the mining company to supply a place of worship for the predominantly Catholic, Eastern European miners. The church's name honored the patron saint of miners. During Thurber's peak in the early 1900s, confessions were heard in six different languages. In 1894, a school was added alongside the church. It closed in 1923, at which time it still had six nuns serving 168 students. In 1941, the vacant church was cut in half and hauled to Mingus, but in 1993, it was relocated back to Thurber and restored as a nondenominational church.

Time has been unkind to these weather-battered, wooden buildings sandwiching a habitable home in Elkhorn, Montana. However, time has created personality. The loss of shingles, windows, doors, and wooden siding boards allows rain and snow to enter; the lack of proper foundations, maintenance, and paint, as well as poor construction practices, cause buildings to deteriorate rapidly or tilt awkwardly one way or another. Wood begins to curl, pulling loose from the nails binding it together; shingles slide off roofs; and encroaching greenery assaults the structures. Thus, another ghost town gains character. Since wood was one of the least expensive building materials in the Northwest, many of the region's ghost towns exhibit either log or sawn-wood buildings. However, with the weather generally being wetter in that part of the country, unused buildings age quickly.

The Northwestern States

The five northwestern states of Washington, Oregon, Idaho, Montana, and Wyoming offer ghost-town lovers a huge variety of places to explore. From mining to fishing, from logging to ranching, from forts to railroad boomtowns, an array of ghost towns lie scattered across nearly half a million square miles of forests, plains, and mountains. These places vary from barren, long-forgotten sites to faded but still living towns.

This is the landscape traversed from 1803 to 1806 by Lewis and Clark's Corps of Discovery and 42 years later by the Oregon Trail. Beaver hunters, mountain men, and gold miners opened the country. Log forts along the seacoast, silver mining camps perched on high rocky cliffs in the interior mountains, and lonely railroad boomtowns on Wyoming's High Plains all anchored civilization, leaving thousands of unique and interesting places to explore.

An Influx of Settlers

Settlement of the Northwest was slow. After Lewis and Clark, the first wave of explorers washed over the region from approximately 1810 until 1840. These fur trappers and traders spread across the region in search of beaver. In 1841, however, with the rapid demise of demand for beaver pelts, they dispersed, leaving the area to new settlers drawn to Oregon's rich-soiled Willamette Valley. Stretching from present-day Eugene north to Portland, this valley was the focus of an 1840s land rush to Oregon and the final destination for more than

50,000 settlers who braved the four- to six-month, 2,000-mile journey from the area around Independence, Missouri.

During this time, the territory was jointly controlled by the United States and Britain, but in 1846, the region came completely under U.S. jurisdiction. In 1848, the discovery of gold in California created a sudden national interest in gold mining. Some 200,000 travelers trekked west across the Oregon Trail, with many turning south into the California gold fields. A string of military posts were established within eyeshot of the road to help protect and sell provisions to travelers.

By the early 1850s, the initial excitement of the Gold Rush had worn off, and a strong interest in prospecting for precious metals across the Northwest created periodic ripples of interest when rich lodes of gold or silver were discovered. Unlike the Southwest, however, there was no discernible pattern to the rushes.

Headstones stand askew while surrounding rock walls collapse due to neglect in this once well-kept but now-forgotten cemetery in Silver City, Idaho.

A Diversity of Livelihoods

Once the mining booms settled down, folks focused on the richness of the region's soil and water. The banks of the lower Columbia River were lined with small fishing villages, and canneries popped up along with supporting camps and towns. Stretching east of the Cascade Mountains into the far eastern plains, agriculture took hold. Farming and cattle towns were established, most flourishing through the middle of the 1900s. Gold and silver mining spread east into the upper Rockies and other mountain ranges in Idaho, Wyoming, and western Montana. In the late 1800s, the grassy plains of Montana and Wyoming supported large ranches. Logging spread rapidly throughout the forested regions, where ephemeral logging camps sprouted like weeds in a tilled field.

With all these new points of civilization popping up all over, the need for coal, transportation, and other commodities increased. Railroad lines pushed across the landscape, bringing construction camps, stations, railroad repair facilities, and towns to support those activities. Fuel was needed for the trains, so coal mining became big business, especially in southern Wyoming and the hills south of Seattle. Military posts remained, but many, such as Fort Laramie, Wyoming, for example, began to serve the civilian traveler population. These former forts became bustling trading posts and travel supply centers, a far cry from their original intent of providing military defense and offense.

A Changing Region

As the 20th century reached its midpoint, the need for the high number of tiny towns began to fade, especially in the agricultural realm. Chesterfield, Idaho, and Jay Em, Wyoming, are two good examples of these dead agricultural communities. Mechanization of farming, long-distance vehicles that allowed more freedom of movement, and the switching of trains from coal to diesel power all caused a demise in the need for so many of these scattered communities. The fishing and logging industries also became more up-to-date, losing their dependence on local support camps housing and providing for the workers.

As the post–World War II Northwest modernized, growth in the urban areas of Oregon and Washington usurped the need for single-economy towns. Such communities faded, becoming ghost towns and changing small-town America's character.

Exploring Ghost Towns

The Northwest is home to weather extremes. Western Oregon and Washington get a *lot* of rain! From the Cascades to the Rocky Mountains at the far edge of Idaho, however, the northern Great Basin is blessed with hot, dry summers as well as brutally cold winters. On the flip side of the Rockies, stretching east to the nether reaches of Montana and Wyoming's plains, the shadow of the mountain range gives rise to the massive sea of grass known as the Great Plains.

In the Northwest, clusters of ghost towns appear scattered almost randomly, yet they are often linked by economic bases. They can lurk in the thick pine forests of the mountains, hide in the tall prairie grass of the plains, or squat comfortably tucked into the corrugated landscape of the Great Basin.

Because extreme weather conditions and wooden structures don't mix well, tangible ghost towns are less common here than in the Southwest. Even so, a tremendous variety of ghost towns encourages exploration. Some are accessible by paved roads, while others require four-wheel drive to reach them. Some are being restored, while a few remain picturesque jumbles of wooden buildings. In this land of variety, all are eager to share their story.

Abandoned and alone, this ghostly real estate office building in Molson, Washington, is slowly being reclaimed by the lush greenery nurtured by the abundant rain and snow of the Northwest.

No more dust. No more wagons delivering raw ore and then leaving with gold bullion. No more incessant pounding of massive iron stamps. This former gold mill in Nighthawk, Washington, now only whispers of the past. Loose boards flap in the breeze, birds call to each other from the dark recesses of shelter, and the tin roof echoes the sound of drumming raindrops across the valley. Abandoned, forgotten, and full of character, this milling complex is fading as fast as the town and the mine it once supported.

Bodie, Washington

This classic old gold mining and milling town is located along Toroda Creek about 15 miles north-northeast of Wauconda. The original gold discoveries were made around 1888 a mile north of the confluence of Toroda and Bodie creeks by Henry Dewitz. His discovery caused a minor rush, and by 1890, a small mining camp had been established at the mouth of Bodie Creek. The name Bodie attached itself to the camp by 1896. In 1900, the camp relocated closer to the mine. A sawmill was also established at the mine site.

The town consisted of wood and log buildings holding businesses such as an assay office, a blacksmith, a bunkhouse, a cookhouse, a general store, a hotel, a livery, a restaurant, and a school. The latter is said to have also housed a saloon and an apartment after it was no longer used as an institution of learning.

Dewitz and his brother sold their mine to the Wrigley brothers, who in 1902 built a large reduction mill at the mine site. That mill building was intentionally burned in 1962. Bodie itself continued to prosper until 1917, when the Bodie Mine closed. The town quickly followed suit. Then in the mid-1930s, prospectors came back, and Bodie operated until 1942, producing $1.25 million in gold. About half a dozen buildings still stand today at this road-accessible ghost town.

Located on the side of the hill southeast of the town site of Bodie, the Bodie Mine and Mill were the heart and soul of the town's economic life. This photograph of the Bodie Mill, likely taken shortly before the Second World War, shows the extent of the workings. The reduction mill was built by the Wrigley brothers in 1902 and operated until 1942. After its closure in World War II, it never reopened, and it was burned in 1962. The structure is currently idle but under claim.

Top: The log cabin on the left is said to have been built by Henry Dewitz in 1896. Dewitz made the original gold discoveries that gave birth to this old mining town. Several other cabins are tucked back in the trees. *Above:* Across Toroda Creek Road from the Dewitz cabin and sitting adjacent to the highway is this rickety, old, two-story wooden structure that has been called both the Bodie Store and the Bodie Hotel. It has also served as a school, with the classrooms on the first floor and a teacher's apartment above. Once the school was no longer needed, so it's been claimed, the building was turned into a saloon.

Logging and Fishing Camps of the Northwest

IN ADDITION TO its mining heritage, the Pacific Northwest hosted hundreds of lumber camps and fishing villages, most of which are long gone and long forgotten. The lumber camps can be divided between unnamed, temporary tent camps following the lumber operation through the forests and permanent settlements located around sawmills and shipping ports. The latter usually lasted long enough to find a place on maps. Many of these are still living, or if ghosted, have tangible ruins. Places such as Port Blakely, Washington, still have foundations and pilings from the wharves. Others, such as Port Gamble, Washington, have been transformed into living, modern, heritage-proud communities.

Along the lower Columbia River, numerous fishing villages and cannery towns stuck wooden noses out over the fish-filled waters. Skamokawa, Washington, is an example of a still-living, semi-ghost fishing town filled with quaint, colorful, picturesque buildings. It is much smaller than it was in its glory days, though. Other locations, such as Mayger, Oregon, are just a few empty old buildings sitting on unstable wharves perched precariously over the temperamental river. Many others have washed away, their sites forgotten and lost to time, known only to a few.

Molson, Washington

Molson holds an interesting footnote among ghost towns: It was three overlapping town sites that were all occupied at the same time. Molson was established around 1900 about two miles south of the Canadian border, and northeast of Oroville. George Meacham and financier John Molson (of the Canadian brewing family) funded the development as well as the Poland China Gold Mine, which was five miles east.

A town was platted, lots sold, and buildings built, including three general stores, three saloons, and the massive, wooden three-story Hotel Tonasket. In June 1901, however, Molson and Meacham pulled their money. Only 13 people remained where 300 had formerly lived.

But homesteaders soon arrived, and within a couple of years, stores reopened and some life returned. The Molson Townsite Company began redevelopment as rumors of a coming railroad gave the town the familiar feel of boom. But then J. H. McDonald filed for a homestead on land that included a portion of the redeveloping Molson. On April 15, 1909, he posted a notice to vacate on that portion encroaching on his land. Litigation quickly followed.

The Molson storekeeper relocated to the railroad and was followed by the rest of the folks on McDonald's land. New Molson was born. For years, residents of Old and New bickered and fought. If a store would open at the site of one town, the other wanted one, too. Then in 1914, a school was built dead center between them. Center Molson was born.

It wasn't long after that, however, that the railroad was removed and all three parts of Molson folded. The last store closed in 1955. Numerous buildings, including museums, remain at all three sites.

The sign on the building says, "Ye Olde Molson—1900." It sits upon the original Molson State Bank building. To the right of the bank is the Poland China and Molson Gold Mines Company assay office, which was moved from the mine into Old Molson. Most of the buildings standing in Old Molson have been restored, relocated, or accurately rebuilt. The town's buildings and assorted other structures, along with all the gathered-up relics, make up an exciting open-air museum filled with the tangible history of this three-part town. Just up the road are the two remaining brick structures of Center Molson. And New Molson, with its cluster of buildings and 35 residents, lies about a quarter mile north of Center Molson. From one end to the other, all three parts of the entire town stretch about half a mile.

Below: The faded sign at the top of this restored false front in Old Molson says, "Law and Order of the Highlands 1896–1972," while the lower sign reads, "Charles Dvorak Atty 1908–1910." The region around Molson is affectionately called "The Highlands" due to its elevation.

Above left: Old Molson consists of a handful of ancient wooden buildings and many relics of the days when the three Molsons were bustling. In addition to the mining industry, scattered farms added to the economic support of the entire community. This sign most likely came from a farm implement dealer in New Molson. *Above:* The Molson State Bank has a unique angled entrance. When the building was originally built, it was placed on skids so it could be dragged from lot to lot as litigation over the original town's site unfolded. Inside the bank is a two-windowed, wooden teller's cage, an old safe, and other relics of past financial days.

This view looks north across the southwestern corner of Nighthawk. On the left is the Similkameen River bridge. The former railroad came through in front of these buildings, just out of the picture on the right. The two-story building with the red door is claimed by some to have been a house of ill repute, built around 1903. The structure on the left was once a livery stable—it was built by Doc Andrus at around the same time.

Nighthawk, Washington

Nighthawk was named after a bird common to the area. It wasn't a mining town per se, but a mining supply and transportation center that grew up around a ferry on the south side of the Similkameen River, 12 miles northwest of Oroville and five miles south of the Canadian border. The town got its start around 1900, and when the railroad reached it, it became a booming mining supply center.

In 1903, some of the local businesses included a brothel, a freighting company office, a general store, the two-story Nighthawk Hotel built by Ed McNull, a livery stable, a railroad depot, and several saloons. A small U.S. Customs Office may also have been present, although it is unclear whether this was at the town or if it was the same one that currently sits five miles to the north on the U.S./Canada border. The Nighthawk Mine perched on the side of a hill just south of town.

By the 1950s Nighthawk had faded, and the train was down to a couple of stops a week. The tracks were pulled out that same decade. By the 1970s, only the small general store remained in operation. Today Nighthawk is a photogenic collection of buildings, including the old two-story hotel, the schoolhouse, and cabins.

Right: The Nighthawk General Store also housed the post office and a Mobil gas station in 1969. By 2001, it had been converted into a private residence.

Above left: This old house is located at the Kaaba-Texas Mine, about a mile south of Nighthawk, along the west side of Allemandi Road and the Similkameen River. *Above:* The Nighthawk Hotel was built in 1903 to serve those traveling to and from the mines in the area. It was much larger than most small towns with only 50 residents would require, yet it was well used. Partially burned in 1910, the hotel was rebuilt and later served as a boarding house for miners at the Nighthawk Mine. Once the mines slowed and the railroad stopped running, the old hotel boarded only ghosts.

Golden, Oregon

Golden, Oregon, is one of the earliest Western mining camps established as the California Gold Rush began. It was actually part of the mining boom that enveloped northwestern California and southwestern Oregon in 1850, the year the original placer gold deposits were discovered along Coyote Creek, about four miles east of today's Interstate 5 and just north of the Oregon/California state line.

The resources were quickly drained, and the boomers headed off to other, more promising locations along the Salmon River. Some 500 Chinese miners then moved onto the old placer workings and patiently panned and removed the remaining gold. When the Salmon River operations folded, however, many of the previous miners came back. The Chinese then either sold their claims back to the original miners or, as some sources contend, were forced off their claims.

Around 1892 enough people were in the area to establish a small town. A church, a carriage house, and a general store began operation. Four years later a school was built and was followed by the post office, which was in operation from 1896 until 1920. Even though there were 200 people, however, there were no saloons.

By the 1920s, Golden began to limp, its energy gone and its economy in tatters. Today, the town is slowly being restored. Some of that restoration will include reconstruction of buildings no longer standing.

Right: The Golden Mercantile also housed the town's post office. It was typical in smaller communities for the post office to operate from a corner of the general store or the lobby of a hotel rather than in its own stand-alone structure. Now restored, this store is one of four buildings in the Golden State Heritage Site and Historic District. It is owned and administered by the Oregon Parks and Recreation Department. All four restored buildings were also added to the National Register of Historic Places in 2002.

Above: The Golden Mercantile store was built around 1896 by Schuyler Ruble. He sold to Columbus Bennett, who then sold to Harold McIntosh. This photo of the rear of the store was probably taken between 1956 and 1968, when Blue Chip Stamps were given out.

The Golden Community Church (seen in better days with a white paint job in the undated photo at left and in the present day above) was originally built around 1892 by Reverend William N. Ruble (Schuyler's brother) and his wife, Sarah McKay Ruble. Ruble was a carpenter and a recently accredited Campbellite pastor. The Campbellites were a revivalist offshoot of the Presbyterian Church founded by Thomas Campbell in the early 1800s, and they evolved into today's Church of Christ. Shortly after this building was dedicated, it became the Free Methodist church. Although it was one of two churches in town, it was the only church building. The other congregation had no building but met in the town's schoolhouse a short distance away. Today, this restored church is open to the public and used for weddings and other events.

Hardman, Oregon

This little agricultural ghost in north-central Oregon sits at the southern edge of the grasslands in southwestern Morrow County. It was the winner in a post office free-for-all scrap between a pair of "dogtowns." According to Lambert Florin in *Oregon Ghost Towns,* Raw Dog (which was originally called Dairyville) and Yellow Dog were rival stage stations a mile apart. In the 1870s, stages and various wagon trains would, depending on the driver's preferences, stop at either town. By the late 1870s, rumors of a coming post office caused the rivalry to increase. Since Raw Dog was a bit bigger, the dogfight ended when the post office landed there in 1881. However, the postal authorities didn't like the name, so the post office was named after David Hardman, the landowner on whose farm the building was located.

Hardman grew, adding a hotel, an Independent Order of Odd Fellows (IOOF) Hall, a jail, a flour mill, a drugstore, a grocery store, churches, a school, and a community water pump, among other businesses. The town is said to have had 900 residents in the 1880s.

As time moved forward, Hardman faded, becoming just a small cluster of abandoned buildings and a handful of people along the highway. In 1968 the last business shut down. The Hardman Historical Society now operates out of the restored IOOF Hall. In his book *Oregon for the Curious*, Ralph Friedman calls Hardman "a ghost town so ghostly it almost makes you shudder."

Above: This panoramic view of the once prosperous, bustling, agricultural town of Hardman dates to around 1905. *Left:* Unhindered by endless, nearly treeless grain fields and dead houses with glassless window sockets, eastern Oregon's grassland prairie zephyrs zip through abandoned rooms of farm houses in Hardman. This interestingly designed home is one of many in the area where only memories of yesterday waft away on the winds of time.

A MONUMENT TO THE PAST

With only 20 or so full-time residents in town now, the restored Hardman Community Center (*at left*) is also home to the historical society. It began life in 1870 as the IOOF lodge hall and closed as Hardman faded in the early part of the 20th century. Unlike many of the other buildings in town, however, it remained intact. Up until the 1980s, it was a picturesque, empty hulk sitting alongside the high-way. Downtown Hardman, from its glory days in the 1880s through the struggles of the 1930s, slowly withered in the drying wind. Its businesses closed one at a time, the buildings having fallen down, been torn down, or burned down. Today, throughout town, empty husks of once-thriving businesses, dead cars, windowless houses, and desiccated dreams remain, touching on what once was.

Above: Inside one of the old stores in Hardman, debris and rubble mark where customers once shopped for food, clothing, and other wants and needs. *Left:* The splintering false front and decaying boardwalk at the old general store building lends a unique, desolate, modern-artish air to Hardman's remaining cluster of buildings.

Bonanza, Idaho

Aptly named, Bonanza is located along the Yankee Fork of the Salmon River, nine miles north of Sunbeam, and southwest of Challis. The original gold find here dates to as early as 1866, but despite flurries of discoveries, no boom occurred for a decade. In August 1876, three men found a rich, easy-to-work ledge. The General Custer Mine was staked, then after some brief litigation, the miners sold out for $286,000.

In 1876, Bonanza City began, and the following year it was platted, laid out, and had lots sold.

Log buildings went up, two of the first being a store and a saloon, much to the delight of the local miners. A sawmill was built to supply cut lumber for construction.

By 1880, the population reached somewhere between 600 and 1,500, and the town had a café/dance hall, grocery stores, a hardware store, a hotel, a newspaper (*Yankee Fork Herald*), a post office, saloons, a school, and variety stores. At the General Custer Mine, a 30-stamp mill was completed in 1880, supported by a new town called Custer and its 300 people.

In 1889, a fire swept through Bonanza. Since Custer was growing and thriving, many of the surviving businesses relocated there, and Custer soon counted about 600 residents. Another fire in 1897 sealed Bonanza's fate as a has-been. Custer now had the post office, the people, and the businesses—until 1910, that is, when census found only 12 families to count.

Buildings remain at both Bonanza and Custer. The latter has a museum, and other buildings are being restored.

Bonanza is best known for its handful of wooden buildings and drop-dead gorgeous setting. Relics of the old days range from solid log cabins to rickety wood-frame buildings. The weather-battered buildings found here make for interesting photographs, and thus the town is a magnet for photography buffs. This old cabin is said to have been one of the stores fronting Main Street; after this store closed, it became a private residence. In the 1960s, the long-abandoned structure still had remnants of the rotting boardwalk in front of it.

Above left: Winter in Idaho's mountainous regions can be very cold, as demonstrated by the snow and icicles in this photo of an unidentified gentleman releasing water from behind a local log dam. *Above:* Weathered fencing surrounds a grave in one of the two cemeteries that served both Bonanza and Custer. *Left:* Located near Bonanza and sitting in the Yankee Fork, one of the larger tributaries to the Salmon River, this massive 988-ton dredge mined the river's gravel for gold until 1952. Over its 12-year lifetime, the dredge crept along 5.5 miles of river, processed more than 6.3 million cubic feet of material, and produced more than $1 million in placer gold. Tours of the historic, restored dredge are available.

Chesterfield, Idaho

Chesterfield, Idaho, is a stealth ghost town. Seldom in print, hard to find on the Web yet easy to find on land, it is a true gem. Twenty-seven buildings remain, yet few people visit this town with its permanent population of zero.

Chesterfield's beginning comes with its namesake, a Mormon bishop named Chester Call, who visited the location in 1879. He and his nephew Christian Nelson felt this valley would make an excellent location for a town, so they spread the word, and a little town quickly developed. The two earliest structures here were a community meetinghouse and a nearby sawmill. Only four years later, Chesterfield had been surveyed, and lots had been sold. Construction began, with many of the buildings being built of brick.

In 1890, 339 people lived here. They were supported by a brick kiln, a church, a meetinghouse or community center, a school, a store, a tithing house, and other buildings.

The little community continued to grow, and by 1900, some 418 lived here. Times changed, however, and the town began to fade. Agriculture proved to be extremely tough in this isolated corner of Idaho, and even the self-reliant Mormons began to experience crop difficulties. Through the early 1900s, Chesterfield continued its slow decline.

Walking the streets of this former community brings alive the dreams and aspirations of these pioneers. Life was tough here, but they had family and friends to lean on. They stuck together and survived—for a while. Chesterfield is in the northern end of the Portneuf Valley, about 30 miles east of Pocatello.

Top: Before restoration began on the dugout home built by Adrian and Katherine Ruger, it was a pile of rocks and lumber and a collapsed hole. *Above*: The Rugers arrived in Chesterfield around 1900, building their home by partially digging into the ground to save on construction costs. In 2009, reconstruction began, to be completed in summer 2010.

In 1999 when this photo was taken, the former Amusement Hall was just a pile of bricks, a wooden sign, and greenery. It was originally built in 1895, serving as Chesterfield's community center, a place where dances, weddings, and other social and recreational activities took place. The single-story brick building had a hardwood floor, a stage, benches along the walls, and a potbellied stove in the corner for warmth. By the 1960s it had become structurally unsound, so it was torn down. Many years later, it was rebuilt from original bricks on site. Plans for the new building were drawn from period photos, with all dimensions scaled by counting bricks. Construction was done by volunteers and completed in 2006. The rebuilt hall (*at far left*) again serves as the ghost town's community center.

Moses and Mary Muir built this brick home in 1888, which makes it Chesterfield's oldest documented brick house. In the style of the day, there were two front doors protected by a large covered porch, whose faint outline can still be seen on the front of the house. The long-gone porch's railing supports matched the porch columns with turned shafts, squared bases, and capitals. The column tops had been decorated with curlicue brackets, and along the underside of the porch eave, between the columns, was a filigreed, abacus-like decorative frieze strip. For all of that, however, the rest of the house was devoid of nonessential decoration. Moses and neighbor Charles Higginson owned and operated the small, brick Muir & Higginson Store a block away from their homes.

This substantial brick store building was the last, largest, and best-built of the three general stores in the once-booming little agricultural town of Chesterfield. It was erected in 1903 and owned by Judson Tolman and his son-in-law, Nathan Barlow. After several years, they sold to I. Homer Smith & Sons, who eventually sold out to Joseph Holbrook, who himself ended up operating the store until his death. The Chesterfield post office operated here until the store closed in 1956, and then the building sat vacant for many years. Because it was solid and secure, it was used for storage while other buildings were being restored. Its own turn finally came up in 2009. The store's exterior was renovated, and the interior underwent a complete restoration—accurate even to the correct shade of paint.

In April 1959, the Owyhee Cattlemen's Association held their annual meeting at Silver City. The association has been active since 1878 and still represents more than 200 ranchers in the Owyhee County, Idaho, and the Malheur County, Oregon, areas.

Silver City, Idaho

Near bed-rock, was seen, in pleasing quantities, the idol of avarice, the master of men, and the seductive and winning creature of women—GOLD.

—Quoted in *Gold Camps & Silver Cities* by Merle W. Wells

And so it began. The discovery of a placer deposit of an alloy of gold and silver along Jordan Creek on May 18, 1863, drew in prospectors. The Owyhee Placers, as they were known, were taken up quickly. A year later they were mostly exhausted, and if major deposits of the "idol of avarice" had not been found, they would probably have been forgotten.

On August 15, 1863, however, the Oro Fino quartz ledge was discovered, followed by the Morning Star, a silver ledge. Assays revealed high values. Word got out, and by the spring of 1864, Boonville, Ruby City, and Silver City had become booming mining camps.

The three towns grew quickly, and because Silver City had the best location, it grew the fastest. In 1867 Silver City was awarded the Owyhee County seat, which it held until 1935. This boom continued through the 1870s, and the streets were filled with hundreds of buildings all supporting the thousands of folks that called it home.

Mining booms don't last forever, of course. By 1880 only 600 people remained, and Silver City continued to shrivel until 1942, when the mines closed down. Hands down, Silver City is the best semi-ghost town in Idaho, and one of the best in the country. It is 21 miles southwest of Murphy and 24 miles east of Jordan Valley, Oregon.

This little building announces Silver City to visitors. To the right and behind it is the Masonic Hall, built in 1863. It still houses an active lodge that meets annually in July.

AROUND TOWN

Above: In this view of Silver City from the early 1900s, the dark cluster in the lower right-center is the Idaho Hotel. The school is the light-colored building peeking above the large white Masonic Hall in the center. On the knoll above and to the left of the school is the Catholic church. *Above right:* In 1868, St. Andrew's Catholic Church was established, but the building was sold five years later. A new church building was built in 1882, and St. Andrew's was rededicated as Our Lady of Sorrows. By 1925, the building had fallen into disrepair. As the Episcopal church was shutting down, the congregation donated its still-usable building to the Catholics, which was rededicated in 1928 as Our Lady of Tears. *Right:* In 1863, the massive wooden Idaho Hotel was built in Ruby City, but in 1866 it was dismantled and moved to Silver City. The much-expanded hotel closed around 1942. An abandoned and derelict structure, it was purchased in 1972 by Edward Jagels, who spent the next 30 years restoring it. It is now open, a living monument of Silver City's glory days.

Because of all the still-standing buildings, Elkhorn is one of the best ghost towns in Montana, let alone the country. All but two of the buildings in this state park, however, are privately owned and must be viewed from the street. The two state-owned buildings are open to visitors.

Elkhorn, Montana

Here are the facts: In 1870, silver was discovered nearby. This town grew slowly until the 1880s, when it boomed with churches, hotels, lodge halls, a post office (from 1884 to 1924), 14 saloons, stores, and 2,500 people. The mines faded, finally closing after producing some $14 million in gold and silver.

Sounds like most mining towns, doesn't it? But Elkhorn is a little different—it precisely defines a stereotype. It is a true, classic ghost town filled with wonderfully aged, deep-brown, wooden buildings, some standing and some not-so-standing. Most of the remaining 50 structures are privately owned, and a small handful of residents keep an eye on them. The two best buildings are the two-story lodge halls, which make up Elkhorn State Historic Park.

Elkhorn sits at the end of a long dirt road in a forested bowl southeast of Helena. It boomed through the 1880s and 1890s and wasn't too badly affected by the silver panic of 1893. By the turn of the 20th century, however, life slowed, the mines decreased production, and Elkhorn's boom followed the last outbound train. Because the town has never burned and has always had a few people, what remains makes this a real gem. The buildings are posted and well identified, so visitors can still enjoy them while remaining on the roads.

During Elkhorn's boom years, hundreds of woodcutters lived at one end of town, their mules bringing in a constant supply of wood to be used as fuel to keep residents warm. Massive quantities of wood were also consumed by the silver mines and mills scattered around the hills above town.

Ghost-Town Epidemics

ENGRAVED ON CHILDREN's tombstones in ghost town cemeteries throughout the country are heartbreaking tales of early deaths. The most heart-ripping stories are of epidemics sweeping through, indiscriminately killing off multiple children in a few days or weeks. One cemetery shares the horror of a family losing four children in a three-day period.

Spotty medical care, questionable personal hygiene, and often poor and unsanitary living conditions due to the isolation and ephemeral nature of most of these towns allowed epidemics to rack up high fatality rates, especially in children. In the days before vaccinations, diseases such as typhoid, yellow fever, scarlet fever, diphtheria, influenza, and small pox ripped through early communities, in some cases causing total abandonment.

Graves in the cemetery of Elkhorn, Montana, are heavily skewed toward small children, victims of a diphtheria epidemic in late 1888 and early 1889. Grafton, Utah, was abandoned for a short time after being slammed by diphtheria in January and February 1866, when two families lost six members—five children and one mother. Silverton, Colorado, lost 10 percent of its population, wiped out in the Spanish influenza epidemic of 1918. In Florida and other Southeastern states, yellow fever killed hundreds, forcing a number of towns to be abandoned—forever.

Above Left: On one of Elkhorn's back roads, this sway-backed old cabin is filled with memories of a past life. *Left:* This ancient house is prevented from total collapse only by the grace of the adjoining structure. *Right:* "Here rests the sweetest buds of hope." So reads the epitaph on the tombstone of two young sisters, Beatrice and Clara Roberts. Aged three and a half and five years, respectively, their short lives ended just two days apart, victims of Elkhorn's diphtheria epidemic.

Garnet, Montana

Like Elkhorn, Garnet is a true classic, in this case preserved by the Bureau of Land Management (BLM). This old gold-mining town is located in the Garnet Mountains above Bearmouth, where the original placer gold discoveries were made in 1862 and were followed quickly by the discovery of lode mines. Even though these mines pumped out more than $10 million in gold, the real boom here didn't get underway until the railroad was completed through the canyon below at Bearmouth. Its arrival greatly lessened the cost of transportation.

Garnet's structures of wood and logs were never built to last, most being plopped directly onto the ground without even the benefit of a foundation. And the majority of them *didn't* last, either. Until they decayed away, however, they housed hotels, restaurants, and saloons, as well as enough other businesses to serve a couple thousand people.

Garnet experienced two boom-bust cycles. The first was the decade from 1883 until 1893 when some 1,000 people lived in town and another 3,000 in the hills and valleys around it. The second boom occurred from 1898 through 1904, but by 1905, fewer than 200 people still called it home. A post office opened in 1896, before that second boom, and remained operational until 1928.

In 1912, the town suffered a disastrous fire. As it had already been in decline at that point, the community was never rebuilt, and the fire served as Garnet's funeral pyre. All that remains today is what survived that conflagration.

In 1970, the BLM began restoration of the site to preserve the 40 structures still standing, allowing visitors a brief taste of the mountain ghost town's gold-mining past.

This is the heart of Garnet today. Kelly's Saloon is the tall false front in left-center. It was originally built sometime before 1898 and sold to L. P. Kelly in October of that year. Kelly's was one of 13 saloons that once operated here. To its right was Frank A. Davey's Garnet General Store, also built around 1898. The large building along the right edge is the J. K. Wells Hotel, built in winter 1897. Behind the hotel and above the rear of the Davey Store is the blacksmith shop.

Left: This interior shows the Wells Hotel, the largest, most impressive building in town. It had a few luxury appointments, such as carved entry doors inset with stained glass windows, a ladies parlor, a large dining room (which was also used for dances and other social functions), and oak staircases. Sanitation was via an exterior outhouse. The accommodations here were cold, as there was no exterior insulation or wall plastering—the only heat came from a couple of potbellied stoves downstairs. The second floor contained private rooms, while the loftlike third floor was a large open dormitory-style room, with lines on the floor to separate the bedrolls of visitors staying in budget accommodations. The hotel closed in the 1930s. Store owner Frank Davey purchased it and moved into the kitchen; when he died in 1947, the hotel and his store were sold, and all merchandise and equipment were auctioned off. *Above:* Like Bodie, California, Garnet's elderly buildings are being stabilized and preserved as is, in a state of arrested decay. The buildings are being made structurally sound, without sacrificing their ghost-town aura.

In the late 1890s, the fading silver-mining town of Granite still sprawled across the hilly terrain above what is now Philipsburg. With some of the richest silver mines in Montana, Granite lived up to its nickname, "The Silver Queen."

Granite, Montana

The chocolate-color, ragged wooden buildings that once housed saloons, general stores, hotels, and several thousand people in Granite mark yet another classic ghost town. The silver here was discovered on July 6, 1875, but there was no development of the mines until 1880.

Granite moved from the category of small mining camp to boomtown in November 1882 with a major silver discovery deep in the Granite Mine. That find precipitated a building spree, when hotels, stores, and blocks of other buildings were added to the town's streetscape. In 1890, Granite had 1,310 people and had to institute water rationing. Two years later, the water problem was solved, and the population had increased to about 3,600. A bank, a brewery, a brothel, four churches, a two-story wooden hospital, various hotels, a three-story miner's union hall, a newspaper, a post office, and 18 saloons lined a long main street. Many of these buildings were open 24 hours a day.

The mine produced $30 million or more in silver, but then came 1893. The Silver Panic closed the mines, and Granite almost disappeared overnight as some 3,000 people headed west toward Philipsburg. At least that's the story. The reality, however, is that the crashing silver markets had already affected the mines, and they had begun slowing before the panic itself. An overnight exit of the town does make a good story, though, even if it's a stretch.

In 1898, a second burst of energy reopened some mines, and Granite enjoyed its second boom. When the mines closed again in 1901, however, Granite was relegated to the past.

Though it looks like a wooden puzzle today, the once-busy Granite Mountain Mining Company mill processed ore from the Ruby Shaft, one of the richest mines in Granite. The massive wooden building once housed a 70-stamp mill, with all its attendant noise and dust. Here millions of dollars worth of silver ore was pulverized by the heavy stamps six days a week.

Left: Only the side and rear walls remain of the Granite Miner's Union Hall. The building was erected in 1890 at a cost of $23,000 to be Granite's social center. It contained meeting rooms for lodges and the Miner's Union, union offices, and a library. Upstairs there was a large open room with a special dance floor for dances, operas, and theatrical productions. Downstairs, miners could enjoy a recreational hall with billiard and card tables. Lighting was provided by oil lamps, a single one of which weighed some 400 pounds. The brick and rock-walled building was hailed in popular 1970s and 1980s ghost-town books as being "solid as a rock." That is no longer the case.

Right: Silence reigns along Granite's Main Street today, a far cry from the noisy, bustling cityscape of the late 1880s. This thoroughfare was once lined with scores of businesses, all designed to separate miners from their money—the Granite Mountain Mining Company giveth (with a little sweat-equity), and the stores, saloons, and other businesses taketh away. The building at the far right is the gutted shell of the Miners Union Hall. On October 4, 1986, the heart and soul of this iconic building was ripped out by a fire caused by vandals. Only charred walls and fond memories remain.

Dead cars, dead buildings, dead grass, dead town: Welcome to Bosler, Wyoming. Abandoned in the early 1970s when the Lincoln Highway was supplanted by Interstate 80, Bosler's buildings languish on the frying pan–flat Wyoming prairie. The seldom-used highway can be seen faintly between the old cabin on the left and the library, which is the large building above the front of the car. The Union Pacific Railroad runs behind the cabin.

Bosler, Wyoming

Bosler's dusty remains lie scattered across both sides of U.S. 30/287 about 20 miles north of Laramie. A few people still keep an eye on the picturesque, unoccupied buildings of this once vibrant town. The identifiable buildings here include the beige library, a brick school, and what appear to be an old motel and an automobile repair garage. The only operating business is Doc's Western Village, a unique collection of merchandise ensconced in a 22,000 square foot, sheet-metal warehouse along the west side of the highway.

The story of Bosler has its share of ups and downs. The town started life as a railroad shipping center and cattle town named after pioneer rancher Frank Bosler. In 1908 a big irrigation project was promised, and the post office, as well as a number of businesses, moved here. When that project turned into vapor, however, the town faded out until the cross-country Lincoln Highway added Bosler to its collection of road towns in the 1920s.

During the 1930s Dust Bowl era, drought hurt the area, and Bosler dried up. But something brought a few people back, as the 1941 population was 264. Unfortunately, the 1941 Works Progress Administration guide doesn't say what may have brought that on, and none of the population figures since 1950 exceed 75 people.

Until Interstate 80 bypassed the town in 1972, Bosler remained a thriving road town with a motel, a restaurant, a gas station, an automotive repair garage, a library, a school, a church, and other assorted businesses. After 1973, however, the Union Pacific closed its Bosler station and loading facility. And Bosler rolled up its sidewalks.

Above left: This former automobile repair garage once serviced the cars of travelers journeying across Wyoming's flat landscape. Today, it is an adjunct to the only business in town, a large whatnot shop that sells most anything. In 1940, a couple hundred folks still lived here, and the roadside services were bustling. *Above:* An old advertisement for Bosler's store appears on what may have been a storage building. *Left:* The Bosler library was housed in this building. It probably closed along with the rest of the town in the early 1970s.

Fort Laramie, Wyoming

There are forts, and then there are *forts*. Fort Laramie is one of the latter. It was more than just a military post, more than a travel destination and supply center. At one time, as the Fort Laramie National Historic Site declares, it was "The Crossroads of a Nation Moving West."

Located along the Oregon, California, Mormon, and Pony Express trails, Fort Laramie was strategically placed. It played an important role in the protection and supply of travelers along those roads as early as 1834 when it was a privately owned fur trading post called Fort William. In 1849 the U.S. government purchased the post and relocated and expanded it into a major military establishment to watch over the 50,000 people a year who used the Platte River trails.

Fort Laramie provided a welcoming travel respite from the rigors of the road, serving as a stagecoach and Pony Express station. The store here supplied travelers, and a post office was also in operation. Major treaties with the Sioux were signed here, and for all the years the fort was a military outpost, it was never attacked—despite the fact that it had no protection beyond traditional fortress walls.

In 1890, the old post was decommissioned, and the land and all the structures were sold at auction to the public. In 1938 the federal government repurchased the property, and Fort Laramie National Monument saw daylight. Restoration began, and in 1960, this became Fort Laramie National Historic Site. It is located on the north side of the Laramie River, south of the North Platte River, and three miles southwest of the present town of Fort Laramie.

Above: From 1834 to 1841, Fort William, also called Fort William-on-the-Laramie, was the only outpost of civilization in this untamed region. Artist Alfred Jacob Miller visited in 1837, and his sketches provide the only visual records of Fort Laramie's original post. *Left:* These are the stabilized ruins of Fort Laramie's 12-bed hospital, which was built in 1873 and closed in 1890.

Left: Facing the north side of the parade field are three clusters of restored buildings. Starting on the left is the colonnaded bachelor officer's quarters that went by the nickname "Old Bedlam." It also served as post headquarters and commander's quarters. Built in 1849, it is the oldest building on post. To its right is the post surgeon's house, a duplex built in 1875. In the same cluster and barely visible is the lieutenant colonel's quarters, and next to that is the post trader's complex. This white and beige building was built in 1850 and sustained several additions. The last building at the far right is the 1874 cavalry barracks.

Right: This is the restored lieutenant colonel's quarters, which was built in 1884. The lieutenant colonel was second in command at Fort Laramie, and his home was one of two nonduplex housing units on post—the commander's quarters was the other. Unlike the other buildings here, this structure was restored while a former resident, the son of the occupants who lived here in 1887 and 1888, was still alive. Although quite elderly, he assisted in design and placement of the interior furnishings, and he donated some of his family's original furniture and other items.

Keeline/Jay Em, Wyoming

Tucked into gentle folds in Wyoming's southeastern prairies are numerous tiny towns, seldom visited, forgotten by life. Most were ranching centers, supporting outlying farms and ranches.

Keeline started as a railroad shipping point for George A. Keeline's 4J Ranch. In 1910 Addison A. Spaugh platted and laid out the town of Keeline, honoring the pioneer rancher. A blacksmith, a post office, a railroad depot school, a store, and two houses comprised the original town. Spaugh brought in a promoter and sold lots, and the town expanded. Some of the new businesses that came included a barbershop, a Chevrolet dealership, a hardware store, a lumberyard, and a restaurant. The *Keeline Record* newspaper was established in 1916 and published until 1923. The population may have reached 440, although evidence of that many people is hard to find in the scattered building shells and ruins that are now watched over by five people.

The town of Jay Em was named after rancher James Moore's *JM* cattle brand. Moore was also once a Pony Express rider, and he settled in the area around 1869. The local post office and store were established in 1915 when they were moved from the ranch. The town once had a newspaper (*Jay Em Sentinel and Fort Laramie News*), a church, an automobile repair garage and gas station, a general store, and other businesses. In the 1930s, a gemstone cutting works was also present. This small ranching center is now a cluster of empty shells maintained and watched over by the 20 or so remaining townsfolk.

Southeastern Wyoming is filled with once-busy little towns that today are ghost or near-ghost towns. This old store and restaurant was located in Hartville, an old mining town located in the same region as Jay Em and Keeline. Hartville still has 70 or so residents along with a main street full of old buildings.

This photo of Keeline circa 1917 shows a much busier little town than visitors will find today. Some of the identifiable businesses include Bushnell's General Merchandise and Coal, Keeline Lumber Company yard, a hardware store, and the Fairview Hotel. Nowadays they are all gone.

SHADOWS FROM OUT OF TIME

One of the few remaining buildings at Keeline is the old school sitting on a low knoll. In 1940, there were still 101 residents, only a quarter of what there had been just 20–30 years before, but still almost 100 more than live there now. Today only the unused shells of the school, the post office, and several cabins and mobile homes remain. The hotel, the old false fronts, the creamery, and all of the town's businesses, including the once-busy sheep-shearing facilities and railroad depot, are all gone. In their day, the local railroad facilities shipped more cream, grain, and hogs than anywhere else along the railroad between Douglas and the Wyoming-Nebraska state line. The original town plat had four "streets" running east-west, and eight "avenues" running north-south.

Left: This water tower base in Jay Em hints at the activity the area once experienced.
Above: The old Wolfe Garage on the left and gas station on the right are two of the identifiable buildings remaining in Jay Em. It operated as the Shoults Garage from 1928 to 1945 and was the Wolfe Garage from 1946 to 1960. Other remaining buildings include the lumber yard, the stone company, the general store, a hardware store, and a bank that operated from 1920 to 1945. On the second floor of these barn-shaped stores was a community hall.

The first floor of this old market building in Galena, Illinois, once bustled with the sounds of commerce (represented by the wagons out front), the sweet smell of baked goods, and colorful items arrayed by various vendors to provide the town's residents a one-stop shopping experience. Not unlike today's indoor flea markets or farmers' markets, market buildings such as this were part of many towns before the Civil War. However, few of them remain. This restored old-timer dates to the mid-1840s and served in its original capacity for nearly seven decades. The upper floor was used for city government, making this a true multipurpose building.

The American Heartland

The central part of the United States is often called the Midwest, the American Breadbasket, or the American Heartland. No matter what it's called, however, it is usually underrepresented in ghost-town literature. But ghost towns abound on the fruited plain where amber fields of grain wave in the ever-present breeze, the undulating prairie that is sliced and diced by meandering, slow-flowing rivers. The Heartland's rich soil is one of the most agriculturally diverse regions in the world. Stretching west from the Ohio River to the western borders of the Dakotas and Nebraska, as well as south from the Canadian border to Oklahoma and Missouri, the area and its agricultural heritage give rise to a bumper crop of ghost towns.

Other than small pockets such as the Black Hills, the tri-state corner southwest of Joplin, Missouri, and the iron and copper country around Lake Superior and Lake Michigan, this is a region richer in agricultural ghost towns than in mining ones. Look at any detailed map of these states: Thousands of tiny marker dots appear—especially in the eight less-urban states west of the Mississippi River. Most of these dots are dying farm towns.

The Big Question

If asked to name the cause of this demise, remaining residents of these sleepy, semi-ghost towns almost uniformly respond: "Big box retailer." Most mom-and-pop grocers, hardware stores, and other retail outlets can't obtain the same price breaks from wholesale suppliers, so their prices are generally higher. As a result, when Joe and Josephine Citizen drive the family jalopy to town to visit "Big Box" for cheaper goods, they will also take care of their banking, dining, and other shopping there. Mom-and-pop gas stations, restaurants, and small-town banks then lose that business, and as their clientele dries up, they eventually end up shutting down. And the cycle continues, customer by customer, store by store, year by year. With the advent of huge corporate-owned megafarms, the numbers of smaller family farms decrease as people flee toward

Slammed by the Great Depression and devastated by the Dust Bowl of the 1930s, many tiny towns in the central states, such as Frontenac, Minnesota (*above*), lost their battle to live as citizens escaped to the cities, leaving behind desiccated hopes and dried-up dreams.

The 1880s through the 1920s were a period of optimistic growth throughout the region. Family farms and supporting towns grew faster in places such as Foss, Oklahoma, than did wheat during a warm spring. Substantial buildings were built, many of which remain as monuments to these hopes.

larger towns and cities. This exodus has resulted in a shrinking demand for schools, churches, and other social outlets in tiny farm towns. Cash-conscious government deems it more cost-effective to consolidate and close schools than to keep them open if they're only half filled. As more folks move away, schools close and church congregations shrink. Many churches find they can no longer support a full-time pastor, so circuit pastors become Sunday-only preachers without roots in the community. Multiple worship services shrink to one per week. Neighboring congregations share buildings and then start to disband, one by one. Abandoned schools and dead churches now share the landscape with block after block of Main Streets filled with empty brick storefronts. A dead town equals a new-born ghost town.

The Shrinking Population

Another regionally common creator of ghost towns is relocation. When some towns were originally established, their placement may have been conveniently located for the local settlers. At a later date, however, when a railroad or high-way was proposed for the area but—due to nearby rivers, steep grades, or even the refusal of landowners to sell, among other reasons—was built miles away, the town's location may have suddenly become less convenient. The new road or railroad

might leave the town quite a distance off the now new-beaten path. Local merchants packed up and moved, rebuilding on or near the transportation corridor, leaving the original town site and most of its buildings to molder and decay.

River ports and railroad centers have been established and abandoned. Copper-, coal-, and iron-mining areas boomed and waned. Logging, relocated county seats, and even utopian colonies grew and died. Each of these added their carcasses to the growing list of ghost towns.

The Heartland's declining rural communities make an interesting study. These scenarios are just a small part of the overall deterioration rural America has experienced since post–World War II prosperity created urban boomtowns and set off a mass migration to the cities. Some of the factors cited here may be more like nails sealing the coffin lid rather than the main event.

Today's Reality

Yesterday's Heartland was in boom. Today's is not. Traveling back roads and scenic byways affords casual travelers plenty of opportunity to experience the real soul of America's Heartland ghosts. Explore towns whose two or three blocks of Main Street are filled with unoccupied buildings. Listen to the ghosts of the past as they whisper stories of hardy pioneers. Smell the clean scent of agriculture wafting on the breeze. Allow the gaze to linger on the weathered bricks of Sacred Heart School. Trace the fading, gilt letters spelling out *Dry Goods & Notions* on the dirty storefront windows of the abandoned Deer Creek Mercantile Company general store. Loll in the shade cast by the sagging wooden canopy, and watch the mama spider weaving her web between the support posts. Focus on the past. Hear the *ka-ching* of the massive brass cash register. Revel in the cheerful shouts and cries of children playing on the now rusty slides and swings at the overgrown park across the street. Listen to farmers talking shop while unloading freshly picked produce at the local market.

Explore and experience the ghost towns of America's Heartland.

Looking uphill toward the east across the southeastern end of Lead, South Dakota, this photo demonstrates the proximity of the headframe of the Homestake Mine. Lead was the main support town for what became America's richest gold mine.

Farm Towns of North Dakota

Scattered across the top of the semi-arid High Plains are hundreds, if not thousands, of dead and dying farm towns barely clinging to life. Decades ago, promises brought people. But the weather and the crashing economy of the 1930s drove them out.

Amidon, Bucyrus, and Gascoyne are just a few of the places now communing with ghosts. Studentless schools, spectral churches, vacant stores, and moneyless shells of banks mark death and abandonment on the wind-blown prairie.

In the early 1900s, railroads and homesteaders created a booming economy with towns popping up all over the prairie. Amidon arrived in 1910, grabbed the county seat of brand-new Slope County in 1915, and quickly boasted a school, banks, churches, a hotel, a restaurant, a movie theater, newspapers, a bowling alley and pool hall, a gas station, an automobile dealer-ship, an undertaker, a barber, a lumberyard, stores of all kinds, and 162 residents in 1930.

Bucyrus began in 1908. Early businesses included a hotel, a restaurant, a Lutheran church, a post office, a bank, a railroad depot, a newspaper, a barber, a drugstore and doctor office, a school, lumberyards, a feed store, various other stores, blacksmiths, and a 1930 population of 124.

Gascoyne was the last of the three, incorporating in 1911. It had grain elevators, a general store, a post office, a school, a lumberyard, a bowling alley, and 97 people in 1930.

Drought, the Dust Bowl, and World War II sucked away employable people. These once-bustling little towns filled with promise are now filled with dead buildings and lost memories in a land that seems to eat its people, eat its buildings, and eat its towns.

Above: Old churches, such as this one in Amidon, dot the North Dakota prairie, many having died due to lack of worshippers. Sometimes the church is the last living building among the ghosts of once-thriving farm towns.
Left: This postcard of Gascoyne was mailed from the town in April 1911. The settlement was originally established along the railroad in 1907 as Fischbein, but the name was changed to Gascoyne in 1908. As growth and prosperity occurred, large homes and a main street lined with businesses quickly gave an air of permanence. The mid-1930s ushered in decline, a state of affairs that has continued to this day. The post office closed in 1982, leaving Gascoyne a hollow shell of what it once had been.

Above: Established in 1883 along the Northern Pacific Railroad, the faded farm town of Driscoll barely hangs in there, south of Interstate 94, east of Bismarck. These grain elevators are the largest structures in town.

Above: Cleveland was founded in June 1882, also along the Northern Pacific Railroad, about 25 miles west of Jamestown. The town grew quickly, adding a post office and other businesses. The ruffle of excitement soon faded, however, and by 1884, Cleveland was a has-been. But in 1900 it was rediscovered: The post office reopened, and the sound of hammers once again echoed across the town. The 1920 census counted 341 residents. Unfortunately, a slow decline began, and by 1930, the population had sagged to 273. In 2008, the Census Bureau estimated only 98 people remaining. Along the west side of Euclid Avenue (Cleveland's main street) is a vacant bank, a grocery store, and the two-story town hall that housed offices upstairs and a dance hall/community center downstairs. *Left:* The building of the Gascoyne Lumber Company is one of the tangible remnants of a former life in this town of 20 or so people.

This view south from Forest Hill circa 1888 shows how large Deadwood grew during its first decade. As the town was isolated and the early population predominately male, Deadwood's wild reputation for violence, saloons, gambling, prostitution, and other vices was well deserved. However, when the railroad arrived in 1890, the isolation ended. The rough element moved on, and Deadwood settled down to a busy, productive life. Despite repeated fires and floods, the town did not die. It has aged gracefully like a fine wine. In 2008, the estimated population was 1,283.

The Black Hills of South Dakota

Gold, gunfighters, and blood! Lakota Sioux, George Armstrong Custer, Calamity Jane, and Wild Bill Hickok! A vivid history filled with colorful personalities enhances the mystique of South Dakota's Black Hills. Substantially more than 1,000 ghost towns have made their appearance in these hills called *Paha Sapa* by the Lakota Sioux. In the summer of 1874, while searching for a location to plant a military post, a party led by Lieutenant Colonel George Armstrong Custer discovered gold. This find created a massive gold rush and conflict with the

Native American inhabitants. It ultimately resulted in Custer and his entire regiment's demise on June 17, 1876, in southeastern Montana, just to the west of the Black Hills.

Once the bottle was uncorked, however, miners swept in, much to the chagrin of the Lakota. In 1875 some 800 white miners were concentrated in three major towns—Custer, Deadwood, and Hill City. A year later, that population had exploded to more than 10,000, for four years of frenzy. Gold was yanked from the ground. Towns popped

up everywhere, disappearing again as the restless miners moved on.

Left today are hundreds of ghost towns with tangible remains. Deadwood was saved from ghostdom by tourists and gambling. Lead (pronounced *leed*) had the magnificent Homestake Mine. Custer and Hill City had location. Other towns, such as Mystic, Rochford, and Central City, are not totally abandoned and offer mini-populations and mini-clusters of colorful buildings.

The Great Homestake Mine

JUST OUTSIDE DEADWOOD and Lead, South Dakota, sits what was America's greatest gold mine. Discovered in 1876 during the Black Hills Gold Rush, this fantastically rich gold mine produced more than 40 million ounces of gold worth more than $1 *billion* during its 126-year lifetime.

In April 1876, three prospectors, Fred and Moses Manuel and Hank Harney, discovered a rich gold vein. As experienced prospectors, they recognized this discovery for what it was—the Big One. They named the mine the Homestake, selling it a year later to California mine investor George Hearst. Hearst and his company owned, or had controlling interests in, a number of major mines, including the two top producers in Nevada's Comstock Lode. Hearst also purchased proper-ties adjacent to the Homestake, obtained water rights, and began production.

The Homestake Mine was the deepest underground mine in the Western Hemisphere, reaching a depth of more than 8,000 feet. Public tours are still conducted of its aboveground milling facilities. In the mid-1990s, its open pit operation was the largest in the country, and the mine produced from both the underground portion and the open pits.

All things eventually end, and the great Homestake Mine shuttered its portals and idled its trucks, and the last miners hung up their hard hats, in January 2002.

Filled with excellent examples of well-tended, late 19th-century architecture, today's Deadwood (*top and above right*) relishes its historic past. In fact, in 1964, the entire city was declared a National Historic Landmark. When gambling was approved (again) in 1989, scores of casinos moved into empty buildings and quickly supplanted mining from the task of bringing in the gold. Revenue obtained from gambling is used by the city to continue its preservation efforts. But lying in the heart of the Black Hills, Mystic (*above left*) is one of several great little ghosts that still have standing buildings. It also has a few ruins, foundations, and historic structures such as this old church building.

McGrew, Nebraska

Like a litter of suckling pigs, a handful of pickup trucks nuzzle against the two-story, pink masonry walls of "The Pink Palace," the only remaining business and downtown hot spot in McGrew, Nebraska. Satellite dishes perched on the roof are out of context with the rest of this town of 99 souls.

In the late morning, birds chirp in trees, vainly trying to cast feeble shade over vacant buildings in the dry husk of what once passed for downtown. The gap-toothed row of empty buildings on Main Street recalls the teens and '20s, an era when McGrew prospered with an automobile dealership and repair garage, a bank, a barbershop, a blacksmith, a butcher, a café, a church, a creamery, several general stores, a grain elevator, a hardware store, a hotel, a lumber and coal yard, a newspaper (called *The Wasp*), a post office, a railroad depot, a saloon, a school, a stockyard, a sugar beet dump, and between 400 and 500 people.

Built in 1920, the magnificent brick school building that once echoed with the excited shouts of children heading out for recess now just amplifies the quiet. The only other buildings in use are the church (built in 1912) and the squat, red-trim, double-door fire station. Everything else, including the 1914 McGrew State Bank, the automotive repair garage, the 1912 McGrew Mercantile Company's General Merchandise block, and the post office (discontinued in 1986) dozes in the warm Nebraska sunshine. Memories hang thick in the air here: memories of when McGrew was a prosperous agricultural community sitting between the railroad and the North Platte River.

Ora Adcock built the McGrew Mercantile Company stores, which today anchor the west side of Main Street, in 1912. The bank building is just out of the frame to the right of the brick store. Adcock opened for business as a general store, expanding and adding new buildings as business increased.

Above: In April 1912, a Presbyterian church was established in McGrew. A building was erected, and services were held until early 1971. The building didn't sit vacant long after that, however, as in May of that year, Platte Valley Bible College lent a hand, and the McGrew Community Church opened its doors. In 1986, it was renamed the Oregon Trail Chapel.

Built in 1914, the former home of the McGrew State Bank is on the west side of Main Street, across from The Pink Palace. In 1917, it was owned by Frank Jones, who also owned a cab service and the local Chevrolet dealership, but the bank failed in 1921. The building has been used for other purposes since.

Within the first decade after being established in 1911, McGrew experienced rapid growth, quickly becoming home to between 400 and 500 people. In that same decade, a large two-story masonry hotel was added to the expanding collection of businesses. Today the hotel no longer operates, but the building has become a popular tavern called the McGrew Lounge, better known as The Pink Palace.

Englewood, Kansas

"Englewood!! The Rose of the Valley... *The Veritable New Chicago of the Great Southwest.*"

Englewood was born in early 1885 with the filing of a plat map, a few buildings, and, as can be seen from the slogan above, much fanfare. Within a year, its list of businesses included drugstores, general stores, grocery stores, hotels, a newspaper, and a restaurant.

Sitting athwart the cattle trail between Texas and Dodge City, Englewood became a must stop for cattle drovers trailing north toward Dodge. Atypical of most cattle towns, the hardest drink *legally* obtainable was cider, but that didn't seem to dampen anyone's spirits.

Collapse walked hand-in-hand with drought and the economic depression of 1893, however. Farmers lost their land. The foreclosing banks failed. Land titles went into disarray. Englewood foundered, and dreams of eclipsing Dodge City disappeared.

In 1906, Colonel Clarence D. Perry offered a portion of his Claremont Ranch to give Englewood a chance at clear-titled rebirth. That offer was accepted by the townsfolk, and a new plat was filed.

Two years later, however, while "New Town" was in the midst of another boom, fire ripped through the entire western half of the business district. Englewood's spirit died with the ashes, its drive destroyed. By 2008, only 95 people remained in New Town. Nearby "Old Town" became a forgotten relic. Englewood's business district has since imploded. The former downtown core straddling a 100-foot-wide dirt main street is in shambles. A few businesses and a post office operate on the periphery, but for "The Veritable New Chicago of the Great Southwest," ghosts are knocking loudly in its empty buildings.

Every "proper" boomtown in the late 1800s boasted of its railroad depot. Even though it was fading by 1896, when this photo was taken, Englewood was no different.

No longer pumping gas, this 1960s-era gas station sits right on the corner of U.S. 283 and Claremont Street, the main street of "New Town." By 2007, the gas pumps shown here had been removed.

Right: Over the years as Englewood faded, the empty, old buildings along both sides of Claremont Street began to crumble. In 1976, the street was almost solidly lined with abandoned brick and rock stores for two blocks. In 1993, about half of them had been torn down. Most of the remaining ones were in a windowless state similar to this former store, which was second from the corner on the north side of Claremont Street, directly across from the gas station shown on the opposite page. *Far right corner:* This stamp displays the postmark of the still-operating Englewood post office.

Left: In this photograph from the early 1900s, Samuel G. Hink stands in front of his single-story Claremont Street shoe repair business. Next door, the center two-story structure houses "Peter Schuttler Wagons." And next door to the left is another two-story building housing an interesting combination of businesses: "H. C. Power & Co., Hardware, Furniture, Undertaking." Today, these early-1900s buildings along the main street of "New Town" are long gone.

Foss, Oklahoma

Off Interstate 40 and west of Clinton, Oklahoma, is a tiny near-dead town. When it was founded in 1900 along Turkey Creek and the railroad, the settlers attempted to name it Graham. When they applied for the post office, however, that name was refused, so they reversed *Graham* to *Maharg*, which was accepted. But in May 1902, Turkey Creek flooded Maharg, destroying buildings and drowning several people. A new location was chosen nearby, on a low rise away from the creek. Once reestablished, the town was renamed Foss after J. M. Foss, a landowner in nearby Cordell.

Within three years, the four-block-square commercial district was filled with businesses such as two banks, a blacksmith, three cotton gins, two drugstores, three dry goods stores, a furniture store/ undertaker, four general stores, three grocers, three hardware stores, three hotels, two restaurants, two saloons, the railroad depot, a post office, and warehouses, along with close to 1,000 people. That number gradually reduced to the 500 range and held steady through the 1920s, with a count of 524 people in 1930. But the Depression and Dust Bowl crippled Foss. It has never recovered.

When I-40 was built, the Route 66 businesses that had kept Foss functioning died, and Foss faded drastically. From 1970 through the 1990s, Foss tallied about 150 people, but those numbers are now falling. The 2000 census tallied only 127. The former business center of town consists of a few buildings, foundation outlines, and weedy sidewalks eerily outlining the now-vacant business blocks.

The J. W. Team cotton gin and office is shown around 1900. This was one of three gin mills operating in Foss around that time.

Above: Memories of road trips, tourism, and Route 66 waft from nearly forgotten, abandoned Kobel's Place south of downtown Foss. Kobel's, which sits under a large tree along the south side of old U.S. Highway 66, is one of the last tangible remains of Foss's good old days. During the heyday of that highway, the gas station, the garage, the café and bar, and the bus station were all wrapped up into one compact, popular stopping place. After Interstate 40 bypassed the town and Route 66 died, Kobel's Place was forgotten and followed Foss into ghost-town heaven. *Right:* This swayback, old cut-stone building in Foss served an unknown purpose, but today it appears to be used for storage. The wood shake roof is failing and beginning to sag; if it is not repaired, it will structurally doom this building.

Picher, Oklahoma

In 1922, Picher was the 13th largest city in Oklahoma. At that time it was eight years old and had 9,676 people. It was also in the heart of the tri-state lead-zinc mining district of Oklahoma, Kansas, and Missouri, southwest of Joplin, Missouri.

Lead-zinc mines were discovered here in 1914. Almost overnight, Picher and Ottawa County became boomtown central. From World War I through the 1920s, when Picher's mines peaked, 50 percent of the world's zinc came from here. The city was interspersed with massive underground mines, mills, and mushrooming piles of mining debris called *chat*. Little attention was given to future environmental concerns.

With World War II and its massive appetite for lead and zinc, Picher's population exploded, possibly reaching 16,000 or even 20,000. After the war, however, mining tanked, and Picher's days seemed to be numbered. The largest mines closed by 1957, and the last little one shut down in 1970.

During the 1990s, elevated lead content was found in the children of Picher. Tar Creek was heavily polluted. Winds stirred up toxic dust clouds from the chat piles, and cave-ins threatened buildings. Weeds, shrubs, and broken windows created an ominous air.

The federal government stepped in, classifying the Picher-Cardin area as a Superfund site. In 2007, the *Washington Post* provided Picher's future epitaph with this headline: "A Tainted Mining Town Dies as Residents Are Paid to Leave."

The 1,640 "lead heads" and "chat rats" counted in 2000 have been evicted, and on June 30, 2009, Picher was officially abandoned. The post office closed in July, and the city was disincorporated on September 1, 2009.

The once-bustling downtown business district lined Connell Avenue in the mining metropolis of Picher, Oklahoma, at its zenith around 1920. Dozens of businesses are visible here, including a hardware store and an automobile repair garage. Faintly visible in the distance are some of the mining company mill buildings.

In addition to a tornado, environmental disaster, and abandonment, Picher also suffers from what might be called "dropsy." Massive sinkholes caused by mine subsidence have opened up, creating serious safety hazards. Get an idea of the size of this hole by comparing it to the person standing on its lip for perspective.

Above: On April 6, 2008, when this photo was taken, Picher was in the process of being abandoned. Once robust, this heavily polluted mining town saw most of its remaining 800 residents waiting for federal buyouts of their properties. The entire city of Picher had been declared a Superfund site for cleaning up uncontrolled hazardous waste due to nearly a century of lead and zinc mining. Most of the buildings had been abandoned as the people left. *Right:* In the late afternoon of May 10, 2008, a tornado with winds estimated in the range of 170 miles per hour ripped through Picher, flattening or extensively damaging some 20 blocks of town, killing six people including a baby, and injuring another 150. A disaster declaration was made, but because of the federal buyouts in progress, no funds were released for repair or rebuilding. Victims of property loss or damage could only use the money for help in relocating.

Frontenac, Minnesota

Sixty miles southeast of St. Paul, along the west side of Lake Pepin, and on the Mississippi River, James "Bully" Wells established an American Indian trading post in 1839. In the 1850s, he sold most of his land to Evert Westervelt. While out hunting, Israel and Lewis Garrard of Cincinnati, Ohio, fell in love with the beauty of this area, and they joined forces with Westervelt in 1857. Together, the three platted and laid out a small town called Westervelt. Two years later, the two Garrards, along with their brothers Kenner and Jeptha, bought out Westervelt and changed the name of their town to Frontenac.

Although interrupted by the Civil War, the brothers ultimately transformed the quiet community into a popular, upscale destination resort. Opulence reigned through the 1870s and 1880s. The majestic three-story Lakeside Hotel, Christ Episcopal Church, and numerous upscale homes were all built, housing high-society vacationers arriving on steamships from as far away as New Orleans.

The railroad was due to come through in the 1870s, but the Garrards refused to sell any land, so Frontenac was bypassed. A station was built a couple of miles away, and the small community that developed around it was christened Frontenac Station. But with the railroad came a decrease in use of steamships, which resulted in diminished river traffic.

In 1901, Israel Garrard passed away, but his legacy continues in the ethereal quiet and beauty of this place. Parts of Frontenac have been designated the only "Historic District" in the state, and much of this area has become Frontenac State Park.

Top: Frontenac Station's main street is U.S. Highway 61/63. These businesses face out onto that road and the railroad across the street. When the highway was built, the community reached out to travelers, offering them numerous services including a small market and a gas station, among other businesses. *Above:* A modern outdoor motorized sports equipment dealership resides in this fancy-fronted antique building that may have had a previous life as an old bank.

REST & RELAXATION

Built in 1867, the majestic Lakeside Hotel was the first of several large hotels built to serve visitors to Frontenac. Originally a two-story warehouse, once the building was remodeled, it became the first resort hotel in that part of the country. Because of the Lakeside Hotel, Frontenac became a magnet for vacationers in the middle-to-late 1800s. In 1870, a large two-story addition was made to the hotel's west side. In addition, five smaller cottages were brought in from elsewhere on the town site and added to the hotel complex. In 1907, a new owner renamed the hotel the Frontenac Inn, operating it as a summer resort until 1937. In 1939, the Methodist Church purchased the property for use as a retreat. It again changed hands in 1987, but due to zoning restrictions, restoration was not completed, and the buildings sat vacant.

Right: Renovation and demolition work continued at the vacant Lakeside Hotel/Frontenac Inn property in 1997 and '98. At that time, one of the cottages, the Virginia Cottage, was relocated from the hotel site to a nearby location from where it had been originally moved; it was then restored into a single-family home. In August 1998, the two-story addition to the Frontenac Inn built in 1870 was demolished, and the hotel converted back to its original three-story configuration. In 2005, another cottage, the Kittle House, was restored for use as a single family residence but was not moved off the property. In early 2009, the old hotel still sat vacant.

Grasston Area, Minnesota

Just west of the line between Pine and Kanabec counties is the tiny incorporated city of Grasston. Still occupied, this is the spectral remains of a once-prosperous agricultural community sitting along the railroad.

Grasston's population has dropped from 229 in 1930 to 105 in 2000, while the commercial district now has more sidewalk and foundations poking out of grassy, vacant lots than it has standing buildings. Grasston was laid out on June 6, 1899, when the railroad came through and built a station. Some of the other businesses in town included a couple of churches, the large 1901 Swan Hotel, a livery stable, a lumberyard, a post office, a school, and other typical small-town businesses. Grasston was also home to a 14-piece band and a men's chorus. The town was incorporated on October 21, 1907.

In 1909, pioneer John Runquist built a large commercial block that contained a bank, a casket company, a confectionary, and a general store on the lower floor. The second floor housed a doctor's office and an opera house. This building burned in 1946.

Today's Grasston contains an empty false front, the post office, the Grasston City Hall, an old gas station that in the late 1990s was converted to a café, a couple of churches, a fire station, an auto repair garage, a feed mill, a grain elevator, and a handful of homes.

Just a few miles to the north is another dying little 100-person farm town named Henriette. It hails from the same era and has a similar number of colorful old buildings remaining from the boom days.

Below left: In the early 1900s, numerous businesses looked out onto Grasston's main street. In this 1910 postcard view, the large building on the right is most likely the Runquist Block that stood from 1909 to 1946.
Below: In this 1974 aerial view of Grasston, the railroad line can faintly be seen just above and parallel to the main highway running diagonally from the upper left to the lower right above the town.

Above: Located north of Grasston, the tiny city of Henriette was established at the same time as Grasston when the Eastern Railway Company of Minnesota ran its tracks through the area in 1898. The little town that developed around the depot was platted in 1901, and buildings were quickly erected. The post office also opened in 1901, and in 1920, the community was incorporated as a village. Today, Henriette still has an active city hall and post office, but most of its other businesses are closed. *Above right:* The present-day fire hall in Grasston replaced an older, white false-front building that still stands but is not being used. *Right:* This abandoned garage in Henriette is one of several unoccupied businesses in town.

Dead Farm Towns in Southwestern Iowa

Lying east of the Missouri River, north of the Missouri state line, and south of Interstate 80 is a lost world. Here in southwestern Iowa, scores of dead and dying farm towns are a microcosm of what's happening throughout America's Heartland.

Each of these towns has its own personality and its own few remaining citizens clinging to hope that the town will somehow come back, reversing a more than 60-year decline. These towns have schools that have been transformed into homes and apartments, stores converted to storage buildings or left empty, and fading advertisements painted on brick walls of long-forgotten stores, hawking forgotten goods and services. Grain silos stand sentinel over decaying main streets where the only active businesses are often the ubiquitous taverns. Rusted-out pickups rattle up and down potholed main streets while bicycles toting kids zip through the dust. Other children play cowboy in weedy, overgrown parks. Ancient, vacant, tree-covered homes sit next door to well-maintained Victorians.

Stretching beyond the ragged edges of dispirited communities, undulating fields of corn march up and down the rolling countryside. Cornfields periodically yield to open space, allowing another tiny town to wallow in its former glory and deepening memories. Two-lane country roads once bringing life-giving commerce flow past faded signs welcoming nonexistent travelers to dead motels, closed stores, and busted banks. Other dead towns sit alongside railroad tracks, no longer even warranting a flag stop for highballing trains. Hope still flickers, and memories flow as thick as Iowa's August air.

Above: The little town of Corley, with its 30 or so residents, sits tucked away in a cluster of trees on the west side of the West Nishnabotna River. A post office operated here from 1880 through 1957, and its most famous structure is this ancient leaning barn.

Mills County German Bank

MINEOLA, - - IOWA

We solicit your business and offer you such facilities as are usually extended by an obliging and carefully managed bank. - - -

Far left: Imogene's population has dropped drastically from 303 in 1930 to about 57 in 2008. The bank and store seen here have long been closed, but a church, a bar and grill, and the post office still operate. *Left:* The Mills County German Bank was established in 1903 to serve the predominantly German population of Mineola and Mills County.

Above: In old Calhoun, a red brick silo stands guard over the ghosts of this long-dead farming town once filled with 200 people. Today, only memories, crumbling ruins, and rubble of the late-1800s boom days remain. *Above right:* Pacific Junction is a slowly fading railroad junction town located just southwest of Glenwood in Mills County. Its large, three-story brick school was built in 1914 and closed in 1986. Pacific Junction still has quite a few people, but the downtown core, with its long row of half-empty, brick buildings, has definitely seen better days. *Right:* This tiny false front, labeled "Hotel," marks Mineola, a little agricultural town whose population hasn't varied much since 1900. Its antique Main Street is lined with whitewashed buildings, some housing active businesses, some turning their empty storefronts out for all to see.

The Death of Heartland Farm Towns

IT´S 1882. THOUSANDS of start-up towns are scattered across the states of America's Heartland, filling this slightly rolling landscape with farms, rich land, farms, bountiful crops, and more farms. From the late 1800s through the 1920s, bustling little agricultural towns exploded across the map. Hundreds of people came to each; businesses arrived and thrived: blacksmiths, schools, churches, restaurants, banks, hotels, newspapers, liveries, hardware stores, farming implement dealers, and many others. But by the early 1930s, prosperity was turning to bust. Towns died by the dozens, hundreds, thousands—from causes already seen throughout this chapter.

Fast-forward to today. In these long-abandoned towns, bank deposits are now only from birds and bats taking refuge inside. The white-painted "Gen'l Mdse" advertisements are barely readable on the side of the still-stately brick stores being overrun by encroaching greenery. The garages haven't serviced a car in 50 years, their rickety, paintless, roofless, wooden buildings soon to be random piles of mocha-colored lumber pieces courtesy of a strong wind gust. Dead vans, rusty sedans, and ancient pickups sit on flattened tires, half-hidden by tall weeds in the old schoolyard. Massive satellite dishes sprout one at a time alongside unmaintained brick schoolhouses, now perhaps home to young, unemployed couples with four sad-faced children.

On sun-baked afternoons and sultry evenings, faded red doors of local taverns witness a brisk business from a good portion of each town's remaining residents—often in only double digits—all toasting their faded dreams and busted hopes.

Ayrshire, Iowa

The roofless, three-story brick hulk of Sacred Heart Catholic School dominates Ayrshire, Iowa. Little traffic stirs the dust covering Main Street's asphalt surface, and the cacophony of cicadas seldom ebbs, as human voices are rare. Stretching across the fertile, rolling green countryside beyond town are corn-raising Century Farms—those of at least 40 acres that have been kept in the same family for 100 years or more—with Irish and German names decorating mailboxes.

The Chicago-Northwestern Railroad breathed life into Ayrshire when it pushed through in 1882. Within two years, 35 people lived here, but that changed quickly, as settlement of Ayrshire ramped up. The population reached 343 in 1930, but it has dropped steadily since, down to an estimated 177 in 2008.

During the 1930s, businesses included at least four churches (Baptist, Catholic, Lutheran, and Methodist-Episcopal), a Catholic school and a public school, two automobile garages, a billiard/beer hall, a blacksmith, a coal and lumber business, a confectioner, a creamery, a drugstore, a farm implements pur-veyor, several gasoline filling stations, two general stores, a furniture store, a grain elevator, grocery stores, a hardware store, a harness shop, a hotel and restaurant, a meat market, a weekly newspaper, a post office, a railroad depot, a stand-alone restau-rant, a telephone exchange, and a baseball team.

Today, only a handful of businesses remain, interspersed with vacant buildings such as the American Legion Hall, a bank, a bar, three of the churches, city hall, the grain elevator, a hair salon, the post office, the telephone company office, and the Silver Lake Township Hall. The public high school built in 1920 closed in the mid-1980s.

Grass growing out of cracks in the sidewalk and the "Closed" signs decorating the doors of empty buildings say it all.

Top: This is the interior of one of Ayrshire's many stores that is no longer in operation. *Above:* Construction of the Sacred Heart Catholic School began in 1920 but wasn't completed until the summer of 1924. The last class was held in 1968.

Above: No longer in use, the First Baptist Church (which was once painted white) now sits in the shade of tall trees. It was built in 1888 and was one of four churches that have served the community. *Above right:* Downtown Ayrshire is home to this brick building that serves two purposes: housing the Ayrshire Office of Laurens State Bank on the left and the post office—in front of the car on the side street—to the right. The bank branch opened in 1931 and ultimately relocated here, leaving an empty shell elsewhere in town. The post office has been in operation since around 1884. *Right:* Sitting along the north side of Silver Lake Avenue, Ayrshire's main street, is a former hardware store that once sold everything from nuts and bolts to hog-oilers and hog-waterers, paints to guns, and tools to tires for Cord automobiles.

Galena, Illinois

Far from being what most folks consider a ghost town, the county seat of Jo Daviess County and a former lead-mining town is nevertheless declining in population as time goes on. At its peak in 1858, Galena was home to 14,000 citizens, a number that dropped to 3,878 in 1930 and to a Census Bureau–estimated 3,333 for 2008.

Galena is a unique, active, historic community fully capitalizing on its historic past. Prior to the Civil War, it was in the heart of America's main lead-mining region. The first lead was shipped from the area's mines in 1816, and a decade later Galena was established. In just one year, 1854, Galena's mines shipped 54 million pounds of lead, more than 80 percent of the country's total!

That same year, however, fire decimated the city. Rebuilding was quick, but a second conflagration in 1856 resulted in the city council passing an ordinance requiring all new buildings to be constructed of brick or stone. As the Civil War wound up, Galena's economy unwound, quickly losing its number-one ranking in the lead-mining industry, in transportation, and in regional marketing. From there, the town rapidly faded through the 1860s.

For the next 100 years, Galena hung in there—barely. Then came the 1960s and early 1970s: City refugees flocked here, liked what they saw, and stayed. Today, Galena's historic district is rated *the* best example of Victorian architecture in the Heartland, with the historic downtown business district having 85 percent of its buildings listed on the National Register of Historic Places. Not a bad legacy!

THE PAST COLORS THE PRESENT

The panorama of Galena in 1915 (*opposite page, top*) displays a vibrant town that has held on to its heritage. Today, more than 1,000 pre-1900 buildings—built mostly of brick and rock like those seen at the bottom of the opposite page—make up the Galena Historic District, which is the heart and soul of this once-bustling lead-mining town. Galena High School (*left*) was built in 1905 to replace a school that had burned. It remained in use until 1980, and in 1985 it was converted into condominiums. The town has a strong religious life, as well. Episcopalians gathered for their first informal church service in 1826. That tiny group grew until 1835, when they formally established Grace Episcopal Church. The congregation rented various buildings until 1849, when they built a magnificent church (*below left*) from locally quarried limestone. In 1859 city clerk Alexander J. Jackson began construction of the home below. In 1865 he sold it to a group of prominent Republican residents who presented it to hometown hero General Ulysses S. Grant, thanking him for his role in winning the Civil War. Before the war, Grant and his family lived in Galena, and he worked in his father's store. Grant and his family lived in this home until 1868, when he was elected president.

This beautiful Italianate mansion was built by Joseph Russell Jones for $30,000 in 1857. He was the secretary-treasurer for the Galena and Minnesota Packet Company. He was also a friend of Ulysses S. Grant, which proved beneficial to him when Grant became president after the Civil War: Grant appointed Jones to be the United States minister to Belgium from 1868 to 1875. Today, tours are offered of the 5,000-square-foot, 22-room, privately owned mansion.

During the early years of rapid growth, commercial districts generally consisted of wood buildings jammed together in a hodgepodge, sometimes mixed with a smattering of rock or brick structures. As a result, fires often leveled entire towns. Galena experienced that unintentional flaming urban renewal in 1854 and 1856. This encouraged the city council to pass an ordinance declaring that when the buildings were rebuilt, they would be built only of brick or stone. As a result of that, even as the town declined, Galena has aged gracefully, its legacy in streets lined with long rows of beautifully aged brick buildings.

Above: This 1915 panoramic view of the Marsden–Black Jack Mine shows the hoist, the mill, and some of the headframes over the mineshafts. This lead-zinc mine is located about three and a half miles south of Galena. It was discovered in 1854 by Stephen Marsden, who was digging a ditch to clear out a spring. The lead-zinc galena ore was called blackjack due to its dark color. At first the zinc interfered with the lead, but in the 1860s, it became a valuable mineral in its own right. Marsden operated his mine until 1877, when he sold it to the Illinois Zinc Company of Peru, Illinois. It operated as the Peru Mine until 1883, during which time it averaged about 325 tons each of zinc and lead. In 1881, the mine employed 125 miners, but it closed in 1883 when zinc prices collapsed. For a short time in 1907 and '08, the Marsden–Black Jack Mining Company operated here, but the mine shut down in 1908, again due to depressed zinc prices. It has had several additional cycles since then of being open and then closed.

This is an 1860s-era painting of Ulysses S. Grant's home, which depicts how it looked during its prime.

Old Shawneetown, Illinois

In the early 1800s, steamboats belching coal smoke and the shouts of thousands dominated the docks at the bustling Ohio River port of Shawneetown, Illinois. Surveyed in 1810, Shawneetown had about 40 log structures early on. In addition to being a busy port of call for Ohio River steamships, it was also a salt-mining center and the Gallatin County seat. Shawneetown had become a powerful commercial, financial, and banking center, with its first bank established in 1816. Shawneetown was also home to a Federal Land Office and was one of two cities actually chartered by the United States government—the other being Washington, D.C.

Due to its riverbank location, however, it was constantly subjected to the whims of the temperamental Ohio. Citizens often had the "pleasure" and added excitement of river water flowing down the streets and into their businesses and homes. In 1937, after decades of off-and-on flooding, the citizens asked for the assistance of the federal government's Works Progress Administration to relocate the town to higher ground.

Thus, Shawneetown was left to the elements and to whomever might want to brave Old Man River and his mercurial moods. The town was reestablished three miles west, with the original site now becoming known as Old Shawneetown. Most of the city's businesses and the Gallatin County seat relocated, making the current Shawneetown home to 1,400 people.

About 250 people remain in Old Shawneetown, which is on State Highway 13, just southwest of the confluence of the Ohio and Wabash rivers where Illinois, Indiana, and Kentucky join.

In late January 1937, unprecedented flooding along the Ohio River washed away towns, killed 385 people, left more than a million people homeless, and caused about half a billion dollars in property damage between Pittsburgh, Pennsylvania, and Cairo, Illinois, which is located at the confluence of the Ohio and the Mississippi rivers. Shawneetown sustained tremendous damage, as can be seen above, and the federal government set up massive tent cities nearby to house the refugees until they could build or relocate (*at top*). As a result of this flood, the physical town of Shawneetown moved to higher ground.

During the depths of America's Great Depression, Shawneetown was seriously damaged by flooding along the Ohio River. Numbers and damaged buildings tell only the statistical, history-book side of the flood. The human side of the tragedy can be seen by the despair deeply etched into the emotionally drained faces of the these helpless, homeless survivors.

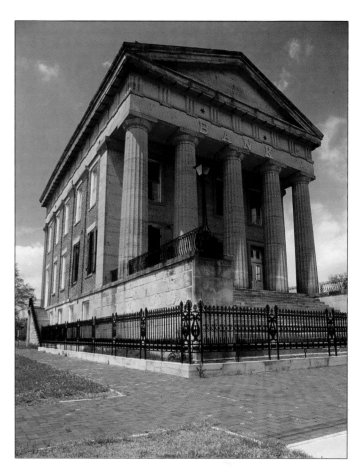

Built between 1839 and 1841, this Greek Revival bank building was constructed of brick and had a limestone front. The Bank of Illinois opened for business in the new structure in 1841 but closed down in 1843. The building remained vacant until 1854, and since that time, it has been home to various banks until it closed for the last time in 1942. It has been vacant since.

John Marshall obtained a charter to open the Bank of Illinois in 1816, and he operated the bank from his home, seen here, until the early 1820s when the bank failed. In 1834, it was reestablished and began operating out of another building in town.

Victoria, Michigan

Ancient copper miners are said to have excavated tons of workable, native copper from Michigan's Upper Peninsula thousands of years ago, leaving no clues as to who they were or where they went. Just before the American Revolution, Alexander Henry came to the area and made an unsuccessful attempt to mine the rich copper that was so pure it could be used raw from the ground.

It wasn't until 1846, however, that a successful attempt was made to extract that copper, and even then, only minor mining occurred until 1899. That was when the boom at the copper mining camp named after England's Queen Victoria began. Miners flocked to the area from all over Europe, including pioneers from Cornwall, Croatia, and Finland.

Victoria was a company mining town financed with English money. The Victoria Mining Company provided 80 cabins, a post office (which opened on September 16, 1899), a general store, and bunkhouses for single miners. Also present were a doctor, a saloon, and a sawmill. Four hundred people lived here in 1905, a number that increased to 750 in 1919.

But when the Victoria mine closed in 1921, the town followed suit, except for the post office, which remained open until December 14, 1935, to serve outlying areas.

Restoration of various structures in the area began in the early 1970s and is ongoing. Guided walking tours are offered for visitors, who may find that the noise of mining has been replaced by the muted quiet of the wind in the ruins of Old Victoria.

Above: In 1967, this two-story brick structure remained near the mine at the old copper mining town. By the mid-1960s, Victoria was almost gone. Forty years of neglect coupled with the brutal winters of the Upper Peninsula had taken their toll. *Left*: In August 1967 this two-story, hand-hewn, log cabin was just a few short years away from being an unidentifiable pile of rotting logs. Log cabin homes such as this were built and furnished to miners and their families by the Victoria Copper Mining Company. Restoration of various buildings in the area began in the 1970s to return them to their 1899 looks. One of the restored cabins, the Arvola house, serves as a museum and visitor center for the historic old mining town.

To date, four buildings at Victoria have been restored and furnished: the Arvola and the Alexander homes, a boarding house, and the Usimaki house for single miners. Other buildings are undergoing restoration. These restorations are so authentic to the time period that it's almost possible to hear the sounds of children playing on the rope swing hanging from the big tree in front of this cabin (*above*). Not only have the cabins in Victoria been restored structurally, they have been furnished accurately to reflect various time periods in the life of the mining camp. The portion of the 1899 Arvola home (*above right*) apart from the visitor center is authentic right down to the wood-burning stove, utensils, and rat trap. The Alexander home is furnished in a style that was popular when the camp shut down. *Right:* This old wooden pipe wrapped in wire once supplied compressed air to the mine from the water-powered, hydraulic compressor plant located near the local dam.

As civilization advanced deeper into the wilderness, small communities were established to service travelers, support logging camps or mining towns, or act as harbingers of a commercial boom in a new location. When industrial towns such as iron furnace communities were established, they were often company owned; the company manager would build large homes, such as this one in Hopewell Furnace, Pennsylvania, to accommodate their comfort.

The Northeastern States

History isn't just a buzzword in the Northeast. It's not just a way of life. It *is* life. Nearly 400 years ago, the Pilgrims established the second successful English settlement in the New World, after Jamestown in the Virginia colony. The present-day city of Plymouth, Massachusetts, traces its roots directly to the Pilgrims' 1620 colony. In nearby Boston, Paul Revere, a silversmith and member of the Sons of Liberty, made history when he established himself as a hero of the American Revolution simply by riding his horse from Charlestown to Lexington to warn of an impending British attack. Ten of the 12 states in this region were part of the original 13 colonies (only Maine and Vermont were not; West Virginia was a part of Virginia).

Of all the regions of the United States, the Northeast is the most difficult in which to find ghost towns. Four hundred years of continual civilization has taken its toll. Land has been claimed, reclaimed, and reclaimed again. Forests have been felled. Communities have sprouted, died, and been plowed over for farming. The fields have been abandoned, forests have returned, and the cycle has continued.

Milling and textile manufacturing towns were established along rivers where small dams were built, impounding water to power the factories and mills. But shifting economies closed the industries, dams were removed, supporting towns died, and the sites were reclaimed by nature. Logging camps, mining towns (yes, mining towns), and a plethora of other types of communities have grown, died, and been forgotten over the passage of nearly four centuries of history.

A Variety of Reasons for Ghost Towns

What these states lack in ghost-town quantity, they make up for in diversity and age. Some of the oldest ghost towns in the country are located here, mainly because, obviously, this was one of the first regions settled by European colonists. This area was also the focus of the American Revolution and the heart of the Second Industrial Revolution. From the War of 1812 until just after the Civil War, the United States of America made use of its great stockpiles of natural resources, its inventiveness, and its desire for self-sufficiency. The previously agrarian American society was transformed into a major urban industrial powerhouse, a change that was focused in the Northeast.

The mid-1800s were a time of massive migration from Europe to the rapidly expanding and strengthening America. Immigrants found ready work in the developing American industrial economy. And more people created the need for more goods and services. Iron forges and furnaces, for instance, increased with the demand for iron and steel products, and coal mining surged to fuel the flames of the furnaces. In the early and mid-1800s, railroads extended their steel tentacles throughout the region. Because coal was needed to power the boilers driving the locomotives, even more coal mining and iron furnaces developed. Those two industries created a previously unknown type of community called a company town—a town that is wholly owned, operated, and controlled by the company that owns the industry supporting the community. That type of control, however, also placed each town at greater risk of ghosthood should the company fail or the economy falter.

In addition to the growth, death, and recycling of land and towns, some of America's oldest cities continue to thrive in this region. New York, established in 1624; Boston, in 1630; Providence, 1636; Philadelphia, 1681; and Baltimore, 1729, are all prosperous cities. There are also hundreds of smaller cities and towns that predate the American Revolution. But, despite the urban nature of the region, forests and mountains cover a large percentage of the area away from the coastal plains. And this is where most of the physical remains of ghost towns lie.

A Different Kind of Ghost Town

Big, brawny Western-style ghost towns do not exist here. Heartland-style faded farm towns filled with complete but abandoned buildings don't exist here, either. Even dead towns filled with roofless building shells aren't found here. What do exist are mostly unidentifiable foundation outlines, cellar holes, and the broken stubs of rock walls hidden in the trees. In a few locations, specific ghost towns have been restored to show visitors what life was like in the pioneering days. Some of these include Batsto, New Jersey, and Hopewell Furnace, Pennsylvania. The ebb and flow of civilization in this small, densely populated region have played havoc on tangible remains. Yet some things do remain; it just takes research and shoe leather to discover them.

Stone, mortar, and locally supplied lumber were used to build solid, substantial buildings. Importing construction materials long distances was nearly unheard of and was extremely expensive, besides. Streams and rivers, then, were utilized to supply water and transportation and to power industry, such as this grist mill anchoring the small town of Batsto, New Jersey.

Deep in the forests of Pennsylvania and West Virginia, coal-mining towns and iron-furnace towns remain. Some have been forgotten, and some have been restored. Faded agricultural towns and fishing villages that flirt with ghosthood line the Piedmont and coastal plains on the eastern side of the Appalachian Mountains. The Pine Barrens of New Jersey support a large number of bog-iron communities, some completely lost and forgotten, some restored. New England has missing mill towns, lost logging camps, forgotten fishing villages, and other communities, now known only to the vapors of the past.

The Northeast was America's front door. Millions of immigrants touched the soil of their new home at crowded immigration stations in New York and Baltimore. Military posts and forts bristled with cannons and massive brick walls, ready to repel any and all invaders. Lighthouses and their tiny self-contained communities dotted sandy and rocky headlands alike, warning ships of danger.

If visits are timed correctly, the curious can have the deserted but restored streets to themselves. Here in History Central, the sounds of ghost commerce, ghost industrialization, and ghost life *can* still be found.

Prosperity, especially among mining and other single-economy towns, was often fleeting. When the economic base was producing, boom times prevailed. Rows of stores competed for business, and towns took pride in their commercial districts. However, once that economic base crumbled, the boom burst and people left, abandoning towns such as Centralia, Pennsylvania (*at left*), to wither and die, their stores vacated and forgotten and their dreams shattered.

Centralia, Pennsylvania

Centralia has become famous over the past 45 or more years for a simple mistake—burning trash in the town landfill. That burn caused the town to be abandoned and, ultimately, wiped off the map. New maps no longer show it at all!

Centralia started out as a typical nondescript northeastern Pennsylvania coal-mining town. Established in 1854 as Centreville, it was renamed Centralia when the post office refused the original name. In 1866 it incorporated as a borough, and for the next hundred years or so it was a bustling anthracite coal–mining town with its population wave following the fortunes of the coal industry. In 1930 there were 2,446 people; in 1980 there were 1,017; and in 2008 only 20 residents still lived there. Since 1984, there has been a mass exodus as the federal and state governments have been booting folks out.

It was all because of the burning dump, which was, unfortunately, located in an abandoned mine pit next to the Independent Order of Odd Fellows Cemetery. On May 27, 1962, the Borough's Fire Department decided to burn trash to rid the area of its "dump smell" for the upcoming Memorial Day Weekend and the increased visits to the cemetery that would come with it. A nice gesture, but...

When the fire burned down to the bottom of the trash layer, it entered an unsealed opening that reached back into the honeycomb of century-old coal-mine tunnels. *Poof!* The seam of underground coal caught fire. Today, that fire continues to burn under Centralia and its last few holdouts.

Top: Downtown Centralia is no longer busy, and most of these commercial buildings along Locust Avenue have been removed. *Above:* Saints Peter and Paul Ukrainian Catholic Church and its adjacent cemetery were located on the hill overlooking Centralia. The church closed as a result of the mine fire in 1985.

Above left: This is one of the few remaining houses out of more than 500 homes that have been demolished. It was one unit in a row of 15 attached houses that once lined its street. *Above:* In the foreground of this photo is one of more than 1,000 vents drilled to allow toxic gases and smoke produced by the underground fire to escape. In the background are a few of Centralia's remaining homes.

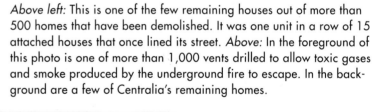

Far left: Fire burning below ground, along with mine subsidence, has buckled State Highway 61. Gaping fissures—some of which can belch toxic smoke—give the old highway an otherworldly, apocalyptic look. The fissured section of the highway south of town has been closed, and a bypass has been built around the problem area. *Left:* This sign is self-explanatory in setting forth the feelings of the remaining locals who have been put out. It also echoes sentiment about the numerous failed attempts to contain and extinguish the fire.

Hopewell Furnace, Pennsylvania

Tucked into the forests of southeastern Pennsylvania, 35 miles northwest of Philadelphia, Hopewell Furnace is one of the best remaining examples of a bygone industry—the charcoal-powered iron forge. Prior to the U.S. Civil War, hundreds of these places dotted the East, helping usher in the American Industrial Revolution.

Hopewell Furnace dates to 1771, when the hardwood charcoal-powered furnace was built to take advantage of iron deposits ten miles south of iron industrialist Mark Bird's existing Hopewell Forge. Bird relocated his Hopewell operations to the new site, building a supporting village around them. In 1772, the furnace produced pots, stove plates, tools, and window-sash weights, as well as cannons and shot for the Continental Army and Navy.

After the Revolutionary War ended, Bird sold the Hopewell furnace, but in 1816, it again produced iron products. Within ten years, production reached about 700 tons a year. The supporting village of Hopewell Furnace had roughly 1,000 people and included businesses and institutions such as a company store, a blacksmith, a livery stable/barn, a wheelwright, the ironmaster's mansion, homes for workers, a church, and a schoolhouse.

Unfortunately for this community, the end for the inefficient charcoal-powered furnaces came around 1850. Production decreased until a flurry of activity occurred during the Civil War, but it slowed again afterward. The fires finally flickered out for good in 1883.

Above: The Ironmaster's Mansion, shown here likely in the mid-1900s, housed the ironmaster and his family. There were also accommodations for their servants and any guests. On the second floor, a study also served as a library and sitting room and was where numerous business transactions occurred. Between 1800 and 1828, the building was constructed in three different phases. *Left:* Four of Hopewell Furnace's 14 restored buildings are shown here. The store, dating to 1784, is on the left. It was a "company store" in that all the needs of the iron plantation workers could be purchased here on credit against their wages. In the center background is the ironmaster's 14-room mansion, which was also known as the "Big House." A barn stretches off to the right, while the smaller Spring House lies beyond it, at the far right edge of the picture. The Spring House served as a "refrigerator," using cold spring water for cooling perishable items.

The Pre–Civil War Iron Industry

PRIOR TO THE American Civil War, a major industry developed to supply the nation with much-needed cast-iron products ranging from nails to stoves to cannonballs. The early cast-iron industry consisted of two types of iron furnaces or forges. One utilized bog iron, while the other used underground or surface-dug iron ore deposits. From the 1700s through the 1860s, most of the furnaces and forges were fired with charcoal, itself a major industry.

The blast furnace process reduced iron ore to a molten liquid, which would be poured into molds to produce various products. Sometimes the molten iron would be cast into iron "pigs" that could later be remelted and cast into products. At first, the industry was heavily concentrated in Massachusetts, New Jersey, and Pennsylvania—by the late 1770s, those areas accounted for one-seventh of the entire world's production.

Almost every colony had its share of ironworks. After the Revolution, the industry expanded into new territories and states, especially the Hanging Rock Iron Region of southern Ohio and northeastern Kentucky, where about 140 furnaces were built. Heavy production also occurred in Alabama, Maryland, and Virginia.

With the end of the Civil War, however, the industry changed. Coal replaced charcoal as fuel. Steel replaced cast-iron, resulting in larger foundries and smelters and eliminating the need for the little iron forges and their support towns. As a result, these towns faded and joined the growing ranks of American ghost towns.

Above: The restored casting shed complex included a large building that sheltered casting operations from the weather. Inside were furnaces and sand casting beds, where pig iron was cast into ingots. Stoves and other cast-iron products were manufactured in another part of the building. Coming into the photo from the upper right is a bridge from the charcoal house, which protected workers from the weather, allowing them to dump charcoal into the furnaces. The small building behind and to the left was the blacksmith shop. *Below:* These are ruins of the former anthracite furnace, which was built in 1849.

Batsto, New Jersey

Deep in the Wharton State Forest in the heart of the Pine Barrens of central New Jersey is a true gem of a ghost town founded before the American Revolution. This town lasted for nearly a century before shutting down.

Charles Read established a charcoal-powered iron forge and village in 1766 to tap the abundant bog iron resources in the Batsto River, as well as in other nearby streams and swamps. In 1773 he sold out to John Cox of Philadelphia, who took over the operation and produced skillets, kettles, pots, and all sorts of household goods. During the Revolutionary War, Batsto's furnaces also produced cannon-balls. After the war and its massive need for iron products ended, other industries such as brickyards, glassworks, a gristmill, and a sawmill also operated here, keeping the village active and growing upward in population to about 1,000.

But like charcoal-powered iron forges elsewhere, the furnaces at Batsto couldn't compete with coal-powered operations. By 1848, they had shut down. The town itself hung in there until 1874 when a fire decimated half of its buildings.

In 1876, Joseph Wharton purchased the property—he farmed the region and operated the sawmill. Finally, in 1954, the state of New Jersey, recognizing the historical aspect of the property, purchased it and established the Wharton State Forest and Batsto State Historic Site. About 40 buildings in the old town have been restored. Today, Batsto is a monument to the perseverance and tenacity of the early ironworkers in America's hinterlands.

Above: The 32-room ironmaster's mansion marks the heart of Batsto. It was originally built for the ironmaster and his family, but after Batsto faded, Joseph Wharton used it to oversee his large estate. Portions of this magnificent home are open for tours. *Right:* Horses and mules were used in the operations here, and they were housed in this restored stone barn, which was built in 1828. Hay was stored above the stalls.

Above: A sawmill is situated at the southern tip of Batsto Lake to cut logs into lumber and shingles for use in the community. The building shown here was built in 1882 and was powered by a water flow that was controlled by the large valves on the dam, visible to the left of the building at the fence line. This mill was built by Joseph Wharton to replace a previous one that dated back to the early days of Batsto. Wharton sold lumber and wooden shingles all over the region, which proved to be a profitable business venture for him. The mill is still usable.

Above: The open latticework and uniquely angled entrance mark the wooden corn crib standing beside the water-powered gristmill, which dates back to 1828. The crib stored much of the corn that was ground in the mill for meal. Other grains were also ground here, and the flour was stored and sold at the nearby on-site general store. *Right:* The gristmill's water-control valve regulated the stream of water entering the mill.

Point Lookout, Maryland

Point Lookout is the southeastern tip of "Mainland" Maryland where the Potomac River dumps into Chesapeake Bay. A lighthouse was constructed at the tip of the point in 1830. Then in 1857, a private resort with a wharf, hotel, and cottages was built.

During the Civil War, the U.S. government leased the area and built Fort Lincoln on the west shore to guard the point. At the very tip of the peninsula, the 1,400-bed Hammond General Hospital was built to treat wounded and sick Union soldiers. It had a round central core with wards radiating outward like wheel spokes.

The existing buildings of the resort were also used by the hospital. On the Chesapeake Bay shoreline, the Army built Camp Hoffman, a prisoner of war "depot." Due to its location away from other towns in Maryland, the entire Point Lookout military complex became a self-sufficient community, not unlike any other community with a single economic base.

The POW Camp was made up of 30 sandy, dead-flat acres surrounded by a 14-foot wooden wall topped by a walkway for armed guards. Between 12,000 and 20,000 prisoners at a time were billeted in tents designed to hold 10,000.

Conditions were miserable and included, at various times, heat, freezing cold, short rations, lack of firewood, rampant disease, flooding, and polluted drinking water.

The camp operated between August 1863 and June 1865, with more than 50,000 prisoners passing through. As many as 4,000 of them died there.

After the war ended, the camp was dismantled. What remains has been reconstructed or restored.

Opposite page: The tip of Point Lookout today is the site for the old lighthouse and a U.S. Navy communication tower. The light is housed in the red turret on top of the two-story building in the foreground.

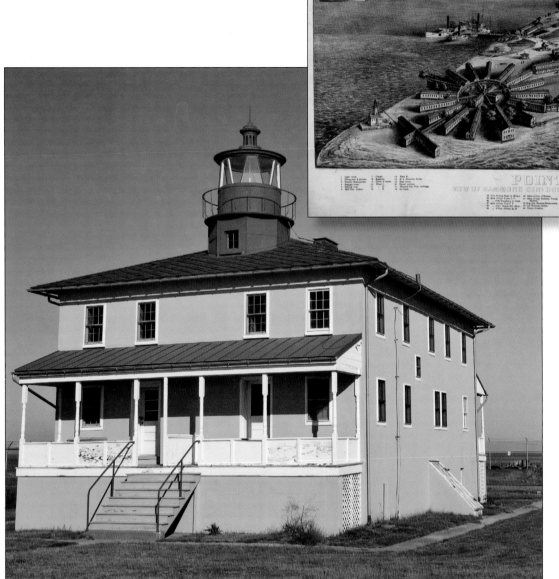

POINT LOOKOUT, M.D.
VIEW OF HAMMOND GEN. HOSPITAL & U.S. GEN. DEPOT FOR PRISONERS OF WAR.

Above: This 1863 lithograph illustrates the facilities at Point Lookout. At the lower left tip is the lighthouse, followed by the wheel-shape Hammond General Hospital. Immediately to the right is the former resort area, reused by the hospital. Wharves are located on the left side of the point directly above the hospital. The fenced area at the upper right is the prisoner of war camp. *Left:* Even though the restored lighthouse is owned by the state of Maryland, it is located behind the fence of the U.S. Naval Air Test Center. The original single-story lighthouse was built in 1830 and was rebuilt in 1883 when the second floor was added and the light was raised. The building was transferred to the U.S. Coast Guard in 1939, and in 1965 it was deactivated and transferred to the U.S. Navy. Maryland obtained the property in 2002, and the lighthouse was restored in 2007.

Kaymoor, West Virginia

West Virginia was and is coal-mining country. It is also, topography-wise, one of the most wrinkled states. Straight roads and level land are rare, while rivers abound in the bottoms of the creases. North of Beckley, the New River flows through the heart of coal country, cradling numerous coal towns in its bosom.

Kaymoor is one of those towns. Located near Fayetteville, Kaymoor is not just a single coal town but is a cluster of six individual parts—four camps and two mines—all company owned. It was established in 1899, producing coal and coke for the Low Moor Company's iron furnaces in Virginia. Low Moor's properties consisted of two mines midway between gorge rim and bottom, two support towns on the rim, and two shipping centers along the railroad at the bottom, a thousand feet below. The Kaymoor #1 and Kaymoor #2 operations were two miles apart.

The four Kaymoor camps each had their own facilities. "Top" camps were residential while "Bottom" camps contained processing and shipping centers as well as a few residences. Top and bottom camps and midpoint mines were all connected by stairs and an incline haulage tram.

Combined, the Kaymoor camps counted 560 people in 1923. Only half the homes had electricity, while about a fifth had running water. Kaymoor #2 Bottom shut down in the early 1920s, followed by Mine #2 in 1926. Kaymoor then dropped the numbering. In 1935, the coke ovens ceased operation, but the #1 mine survived up and down cycles until 1962. And then, no more Kaymoor.

In 1925 the Low Moor Company sold the Kaymoor operation to the New River & Pocahontas Consolidated Coal Company. The new owner refurbished several buildings, including this coal preparation plant (tipple) located along the railroad. This tipple replaced one that burned in 1924 and had a state of the art washer, dust controller, and sorter, which sorted the coal into four categories: slack, pea stoker, four-inch house coal, and lump. The slack was used as fuel for the coke ovens until they shut down in 1935, and it was then shipped elsewhere. The pea stoker coal was used to fuel Navy ships.

The powder house held the dynamite used in the Kaymoor #1 mine. It was located on the bench level a short distance from the rest of the camp and the mine openings.

This safety board stands at one of the mine entrances at the bench level, 560 feet above the New River and some 400 feet below the rim of the gorge. Note the short height of the mine entrance and the flatness of the coal car on the left. Also located near this entrance were utility buildings and the head-house, which was connected to the tipple and processing buildings at the bottom of the canyon by a tram.

Thurmond, West Virginia

An Amtrak station in a ghost town? Sitting in the heart of West Virginia's New River Gorge coal country, Thurmond is a classic link to the past—a boisterous past when coal and the railroad were king, and the 1920s truly roared.

Imagine a bustling railroad town populated by 500 people and filled with multistory wood, brick, and rock buildings housing banks, stores, and large hotels. Imagine a railroad depot serving 75,000 passengers a year. Imagine all this *without* a main street!

Thurmond was founded in the 1880s along the Chesapeake and Ohio (C&O) Railway. Due to the narrow riverside bench on which the town sat, there was no room for a traditional main street in addition to the railroad. The buildings were all built fronting the town's economic lifeline, with just a narrow walkway between the iron rails and the front doors.

From the 1890s to 1930, Thurmond boomed. In 1930, 482 people lived here, but bust quickly supplanted boom when the massive Dunglen Hotel burned in 1930, followed by failure of the National Bank of Thurmond. As rail traffic slowed, businesses failed. After World War II, railroads switched from coal- to diesel-powered locomotives. Train trips through Thurmond and the gorge decreased, along with the lessened demand for coal. Ultimately, diesel engines became the death of Thurmond's steam engine repair yards, coaling stations, and water tanks. Over the years, fires turned landmarks into memories.

The downtown core, restored railroad depot, church, and a couple dozen homes housing the town's seven people still remain, a classic link to the past.

Top: In November 1988 the former engine house and sand tower of the Chesapeake & Ohio Railway at Thurmond were still standing. The C&O employed hundreds of workers at its Thurmond yards in the early 1900s. The engine house was built around 1902 and expanded about 100 feet in 1921. The large building burned in 1993. *Above*: This is a current view of the railroad station, which was restored in 1995 by the National Park Service. It now serves as Thurmond's visitor center.

Left: Still standing, this concrete coaling tower was built in 1922 to load coal into the tenders of the C&O steam trains. The trains pulled beneath the tower or on the two sides, where chutes were lowered to load the tenders. By 1960, the coal-fired steam engines were gone, and the 500-ton capacity tower was abandoned.

A special train will leave the Dunglen Hotel

Thurmond, West Virginia, at five o'clock

and, returning, will leave Beury at seven o'clock

Please present this card to the conductor

This ticket was issued in the early 1900s for a special excursion train from Thurmond to Beury, a booming, early-1900s coal-mining camp about three miles downriver from Thurmond. Built in 1901, the Dunglen was the leading hotel in Thurmond; it burned in 1930.

Right: The three main buildings in downtown Thurmond today include (*left to right*): the National Bank of Thurmond, the Goodwin-Kincaid Building, and the Mankin Cox Building. The Goodwin-Kincaid was built in 1906, with stores and restaurants as tenants on the first floor. The second floor contained Doctor Ridge's office and an office for the Chesapeake & Potomac Telephone Exchange Company. The upper floors contained apartments. The bank building was built in 1917 and originally housed a jewelry store, a clothing store, and the telegraph office; apartments were above. In 1923, the National Bank of Thurmond moved in—until it failed in the 1930s. Since then, the building has also housed a hotel and restaurant. The Mankin-Cox Building was built in 1904 and housed the Mankin Drug Company and the New River Banking & Trust Company.

Ruins on ruins; shadows of the past paint the gaunt skeleton of this once-stately mansion, still standing more than a century after it last burned. Built in 1750, this picturesque structure in Jamestown, Virginia, was the heart of a mid-18th-century plantation, which itself sat in the midst of ruins from a then 150-year-old colony site. During its long life, the mansion burned three times: once during the Revolutionary War, once during the Civil War, and the last time in 1896.

The Southeastern States

When most Americans think of the southeastern states, the last thing that comes to mind is the idea of ghost towns. But, like the northeastern states, the southeastern states ooze with a colorful history—a very colorful history. America's *first* successful European colony was established here in 1565. Four of the original 13 colonies are located here. Hundreds of ghost towns are also located here.

The state of Florida has the distinction of being the home to America's *oldest* ghost town site as well as its oldest continuously occupied city. The original Spanish colony of Pensacola was established in 1559, but just a few months after that, it was wiped out by a hurricane; two years later it was finally abandoned. In 1565, St. Augustine, America's oldest continuously occupied city, was founded.

The second oldest town site is Charlesfort, South Carolina, located on present-day Parris Island. It was established by the French in 1562 and abandoned the next year. Three years after that, the Spanish founded Santa Elena, a colony and fort at the old French site, which they occupied for more than 20 years until 1587.

The first English colony was Fort Raleigh, North Carolina, which dates to 1584. It failed, but mystery has surrounded that fate ever since. Twenty-three years later, in 1607, the first successful British colony was located at Jamestown, Virginia.

The Scramble for Riches

America's first documented gold mine is also located in the South. The Reed Mine was discovered in southwestern North Carolina in 1799, creating a

Boom, then bust. Boom, then bust. On and on and on. Since the 18th century, this has been the life cycle for thousands of towns across the region. The town's citizens might live a hard-scrabble life, but a select few, due to fortunate circumstances or title, had money. Their prosperity would be shown to all by the construction of great homes, such as the Kirkpatrick Mansion of Cahawba, Alabama. Yet the life cycles of towns ate up the rich as well as the poor, and often these old mansions were vacated when the rest of the towns failed.

limited rush into the area. For the next 30 years, this region was the nation's leading producer of that precious metal, and some 30,000 people have been estimated to have worked those gold fields. In 1828 that all ended with the discovery of gold in the Dahlonega, Georgia, area. Gold fever spread southwest toward northern Alabama and then back up into the Piedmont region of North Carolina and Virginia. In 1848, however, the door slammed shut on Southern gold mines when news of the California Gold Rush electrified the nation.

Many crossroads taverns, also called *ordinaries*, were established along southern pikes, or highways. These travel stops served food and beverages of choice and offered lodging for travelers. Often additional businesses such as general stores, blacksmiths, and liveries established themselves adjacent to the inns, creating the nucleus for a small town. When the country roads were paved and automobiles replaced horses as the main transportation, many of these locations faded and died, especially those located off the main travel routes.

Ghost towns were also created by old ferry crossings, as the Southeast is blessed with many rivers—even if the river crossings were quite often problematic. Enterprising folks established ferries at key locations where busy roads crossed the water, and these spots often came to include an inn or other business designed to serve travelers. Together, these would be the core of another town. When ferries began to be replaced by bridges or were washed away, or when the roads relocated, another ghost town was born.

Left Over from Plantation Culture

Larger sugar and cotton plantations have generally been unknown sources of ghost towns. Small villages were often established in or around the plantations, creating self-supporting communities that housed the workers, either free or slave. The sugar plantations specialized in raising sugarcane, which was rendered into molasses. Since sugarcane is a tropical plant, most such plantations were located in Louisiana or Florida.

After the cotton gin was invented in 1792, cotton became the most lucrative agricultural product in the South, with yields increasing steadily until 1860, at which time the South is said to have produced two-thirds of the world's cotton supply. Like sugar, much of that cotton was produced on huge estates or plantations that were self-contained communities. The rest was grown on smaller farms. But the Civil War changed all that.

After the war ended, slavery was abolished and plantation culture ultimately died, having been replaced by smaller family farms or sharecroppers. Centrally located market and milling towns supported these farms, but even these began to fade out by the 1950s. The biggest cotton producing states were Alabama, Mississippi, and South Carolina.

Other Causes of Ghost Towns

Coal mining in the Appalachian Mountains of Kentucky and Tennessee, as well as on the outer fringes of several other states, began in the early 1800s and continued unabated until the late 1930s. This industry began to fade after the end of World War II, when oil became the energy source of choice and the declining demand for coal killed off hundreds, if not thousands, of Appalachian coal-mining towns. Today, coal is still extensively mined, but company-owned coal-mining camps have slipped into the past.

Then there is the Tennessee Valley Authority. Beginning in the mid-1930s as part of Franklin Roosevelt's New Deal, the TVA built dozens of hydroelectric dams along the Tennessee River system in the western Appalachian region. These massive reservoirs tamed once-wild rivers, but in the process many towns had to be vacated, razed, or relocated. Their old sites are now underwater, mere memories and names on pre-1930s era maps.

Throughout Alabama, Kentucky, Tennessee, and Virginia, iron furnaces developed as early as the 1600s. They really came into their own by the early 1800s with the advent of the American Industrial Revolution. Each of these furnaces supported small self-sufficient towns lasting until most of the furnaces shut down during the Civil War. A few furnaces managed to reopen, but the war pretty much put an end to this kind of small independent operator.

Dixie is filled with ghost towns, many of which have long since become nothing but shadows of the past.

Historical events sometimes become inseparable from the place where those events happened. Whether a particular incident occurred in an entire town or in a single building like this one—the McLean Mansion in Appomattox Court House, Virginia, where the Civil War officially ended—that event becomes synonymous with that structure or location. That one instant in time becomes the focus, while the years, decades, or centuries before and after become lost to the recesses of history. Before and after become irrelevant, forgotten, or both.

Appomattox Court House, Virginia

Manassas Junction, Virginia. July 21, 1861. Retired Army Major Wilmer McLean and his wife Virginia loaned their home to Confederate Brigadier General P.G.T. Beauregard for his headquarters while he planned the first major assault against Union forces gathering nearby. Union cannonballs pummeled the house, and the Civil War's first major battle was underway.

In 1863, the McLeans headed south to another quiet little Virginia town.

One evening—Palm Sunday, April 9, 1865—Wilmer McLean heard a knock at the door. There stood Confederate General Robert E. Lee, who was ushered into the parlor. A half hour later, General Ulysses S. Grant entered the home and was also ushered into the parlor. Appomattox Court House, the tiny, nondescript 20-year-old county seat for Appomattox County, Virginia, with its brick courthouse and handful of other buildings, dozed quietly that Sunday afternoon, its place in American history just having been secured.

A week earlier, the Civil War was closing in on the sleepy Piedmont town with its two blacksmith shops, county jail, law offices, two stables, three stores, a tavern, and homes for 150 or so people. General Lee's Army of Northern Virginia was being dogged by General Grant's boys in blue.

Poor old Wilber McLean. His home at Manassas Junction saw the first major battle of the Civil War. Four years later, the parlor of his home at Appomattox Court House saw the formal end of the war.

Around 1819, the Clover Hill Tavern (*above right*) was established along the Richmond-Lynchburg Stage Coach Road. It served as a way station for travelers, who could obtain food, drink, and overnight accommodations here. In 1845, Appomattox County was formed, and the tiny hamlet of Clover Hill obtained the county seat honors. In true Virginia fashion, the hamlet's name was changed to reflect that stature, and Appomattox Court House was born. A new courthouse (*at left*) was built in 1846 and served as the seat of government until it burned in 1892. At that time, the county seat was shifted three miles to the town of Appomattox, and Appomattox Court House languished in its Civil War fame. The courthouse building was reconstructed in 1964.

Above: On August 1, 1865, two years after purchasing a former tavern built in 1848, the Wilmer McLean family posed on their front porch. Their home had become famous, having served a major role in the formal ending of the Civil War just four months earlier. In 1867, they moved to Prince William County, Virginia, letting this house fall into foreclosure. Various owners rented it out until 1892, when it was dismantled with the failed intent of having it reconstructed and displayed at the 1893 World Columbian Exposition in Chicago. The pile of lumber that had been the house didn't move until 1941, when on-site reconstruction began.

Above: In addition to the main tavern building, the Clover Hill Tavern also had a freestanding guesthouse located on the property. Built at the same time as the main tavern in 1819, this three-story brick structure was graced with exterior balconies and stairs, allowing each room private access. Designed for overflow accommodations, it also had a kitchen, as well as several guest rooms on the first floor; the upper floor and finished attic space were also guest rooms. The guesthouse underwent reconstruction in 1954, with additional rehabilitation occurring in 1997. The main tavern was also rehabilitated in 1954 and underwent preservation in 1995. *Left:* This log outbuilding at the McLean house served as slave quarters during the years the McLean home served as a tavern.

Jamestown, Virginia

After a four-and-a-half-month transatlantic crossing, then two weeks of exploring the coastline for a suitable colony site, three ragtag English ships carrying 104 men and boys landed along the marshy north bank of what would be named the James River in the future colony and state of Virginia. It was May 13, 1607, and the first successful English colony in the New World was about to be established.

The settlers quickly erected a triangular, wood-walled fort and filled it in with English-style buildings constructed of saplings and mud, with thatched roofing. Some of the structures included communal buildings, a church, homes, and storehouses. Life here was no Garden of Eden. The colonists set out gardens, hunted, traded with the local Native Americans, drank bad water, fought mosquitoes, and tried to build a stable life. Despite the arrival of fresh batches of colonists, by the end of 1610, the population had dwindled to 60.

From the summer of 1610 on, however, enough new settlers arrived and new crops were tried that the original investment began to pay off, and the colony expanded. In 1624, the original charter issued to the private Virginia Company was revoked by King James I. He turned Jamestown and Virginia into an English Crown Colony. After 91 years of being at Jamestown, the Virginia colonial capital was switched to the nearby settlement of Williamsburg in 1699. Jamestown was abandoned.

Today, Jamestown's history has been microstudied and archaeologically dissected, and its foundations have been exposed and stabilized. This is truly a unique place. American pride. American history.

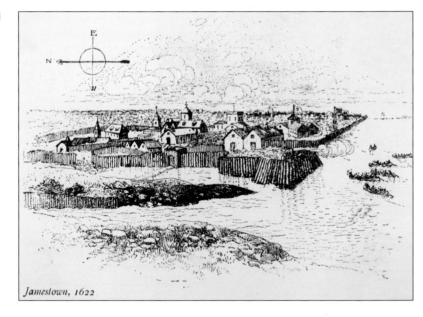

Jamestown, 1622

Above right: This 1622 sketch of Jamestown, which was situated on the north bank of the James River, shows walls, churches, and other buildings stretching off to the far eastern horizon in an idealized view of the colony. In 1624, the population of what was then called James City was only 183. *Right:* Today's Jamestown exists in two parts. The original site, called "Historic Jamestowne," is part of Colonial National Historic Park. Abutting it on the west is "Jamestown Settlement," a living history museum administered by the state of Virginia and consisting of reconstructions of both Jamestown and a Powhatan village populated by period-costumed docents. The thatch-roofed, straw-mud walled buildings have been accurately recreated.

Colonial American Settlements

BEFORE THE AMERICAN Revolution, the part of North America that was to become the United States was rife with exploration, exploitation, and settle-ments from Europe's major power players. As En-gland, France, Holland, Spain, and Sweden jockeyed for dominance in this strange new land filled with natural resources, they confronted nature's moods, were stranded from the homeland by distance, and battled resistance from the native inhabitants.

For the most part, the earliest colonies were unsuccessful. Yet the Europeans persevered. Successful beachhead colonies were finally estab-lished, and a future nation was conceived. In most cases, the colonies were founded for economic reasons, the nations establishing them seeking products to benefit the homeland. By establishing colonies, and eventually forts, the European colo-nizers could lay claim to the land and its future economic benefit, as well as protect it from interlopers—or other colonizing nations.

As time went on, the Spanish settled the south-western area, establishing strings of missions throughout California, Arizona, New Mexico, and Texas. They also established settlements in Florida and the Southeast. The French colonized Louisiana and the Mississippi River region through the heart of the continent. The English set their colonies along the coastal rim from Maine south to Georgia. The Swedes and Dutch filled in the mid-Atlantic region, but they were each squeezed out by the English by the 1670s.

Inarguably, the single most successful colony established by any of the colonial powers was the original Dutch colonial capital at New Amsterdam. When the English took over, they renamed it New York City.

The weathered brick ruin of Jamestown's church tower is the only original structure remaining above ground at the original colony site. This tower is all that is left of the brick church built in 1676 to replace a series of churches on the same site, the last of which had been burned during Bacon's Rebellion that year. The 1676 church was used until about 1750, when it was abandoned. In 1893, the Association for the Preservation of Virginia Antiquities obtained the property and preserved the tower in its 1893 condition. The Jamestown Memorial Church abutting it was built in 1906 in celebration of Jamestown's 300th anniversary. This is not a consecrated church but serves more as a memorial chapel, hosting weddings and other events. The historical importance of Jamestown's 400th birthday was not lost on the state of Virginia, which celebrated the occasion on a special series of license plates.

Barthell and Blue Heron, Kentucky

During the early 1900s, the Stearns Coal & Lumber Company operated a number of mines and mining camps from their headquarters at Stearns, Kentucky. Mines #1 and #2 supported the camp of Barthell, while Mine #18 supported the small camp of Blue Heron.

The Stearns Mines #1 and #2 at Barthell began operation in 1903, and the camp was built at that time. A little "disagreement" over union or nonunion mining resulted in the hotel being burned in 1908.

Up through the 1930s, Barthell had at least 200 miners and a number of buildings, including a company store, a post office, a railroad depot, a combined church and school, a doctor's office, a barbershop, and a bathhouse. In 1943, Mine #1 closed after the coal-loading plant and neighboring buildings burned and weren't replaced. In 1953, Mine #2 closed, and in 1959, the last person left town. A number of Barthell's buildings have been reconstructed to the original plans.

Blue Heron is located southwest of Barthell and once had 300 miners. Mine #18 and the camp that accompanied it operated from 1937 through December 1962. Blue Heron was a small camp, the last owned and operated by the Stearns Company. It consisted of a company store (with post office inside), a railroad depot, a church, a school, a bathhouse, and homes. During the 1980s, a number of these buildings were rebuilt as "ghost structures," empty shells on display to show what the buildings looked like but lacking the "guts." Inside each of these structures, the National Park Service shares the history of life in the old coal-mining camp.

Now a bridge, the former tramway at Blue Heron offers visitors a bird's-eye view of the ghost coal camp. Established by the Michigan-based Stearns Coal and Lumber company, Blue Heron was a typical mid-20th-century company town. The business was headed by Justus Stearns, a Michigan lumber baron, whose company owned more than 200 square miles of virgin forest in southern Kentucky. In 1902, it began coal-mining operations to supplement its lumbering concerns, and the mining payroll quickly exceeded 2,000 miners.

Top: This coal tipple at Blue Heron has been reconstructed. The term *tipple* originally applied to an elevated area where coal cars coming out of a mine were tipped to empty their coal into large bins, but the definition now includes large structures that do that same thing and more. Most of these tipples incorporate conveyor systems and other unloading methods in addition to tipping the mine cars. The coal comes from the mines, via trains, trams, trucks, or conveyor belts. It is next dumped into bins, sorted, cleaned, and prepared for shipping, and then dumped into railroad cars or trucks to be hauled away. This tipple at Blue Heron was one of the most modern processing plants around when it opened in the 1930s, equipped with a 120-ton hopper that received the coal from electric tram cars arriving from the mine via the elevated bridgework. *Left:* Barthell was established in 1902, Stearns Coal and Lumber Company's first mine and mining camp in the area. It quickly developed into a bustling town along Roaring Paunch Creek. This photograph was taken sometime after the Kentucky & Tennessee Railroad arrived in the booming coal camp in 1903.

Cahawba, Alabama

Southwest of Selma, Alabama, at the confluence of the Cahaba and Alabama rivers, is the old town site of Cahawba (also spelled *Cahaba*). Like a cat, this old town has led multiple lives. It began as the first permanent state capital for the state of Alabama and was also the designated county seat for Dallas County.

In the 1820s, a combination of yellow fever and flooding spelled trouble for Cahawba. By just one vote in 1825, the state capital was relocated to Tuscaloosa. Cahawba stumbled but didn't fall.

The resilient citizens saw a bright future as a major river port. Word got out, and new residents kept coming. Rebuilding continued unabated. In 1859, the railroad came through, and some 3,000 people called Cahawba home.

But then the Civil War came to Alabama. Cahawba's railroad was torn up, and a 3,000-person POW camp for captured Union soldiers was established. Nearby Selma was sacked and burned, but Cahawba was spared that indignity when another flood swept through before the Union troops could. But by war's end, Cahawba was nonetheless crippled. Adding insult to injury, the county seat was relocated to a rebuilt Selma in 1866. Reality hit hard. Cahawba was doomed.

During Reconstruction, a nearly abandoned Cahawba revived—somewhat. Former slaves came, turning the town site into an agricultural community filled with family farms. Unfortunately, however, that didn't last. By 1900, the abandoned ruins were becoming one with nature, and by the 1930s little remained.

Today, Cahawba still has enough remaining to make it interesting to visitors. This is real history. Not reconstructed. Not rebuilt.

Top: Between 1858 and 1860, Joseph Babcock built a 15,000-square-foot brick warehouse/cotton shed on top of an old Native American mound above the Alabama River. When the Civil War came to Cahawba, a stockade was built around the building and the property was used to house prisoners of war, holding as many as 3,000 Union soldiers. *Above:* This cabin is not one of Cahawba's older structures, dating only into the early 20th century. It provided a home for some of Cahawba's later citizenry.

Left: This colonnaded home was built by Samuel and Sarah Kirkpatrick during Cahawba's second boom, which started in 1858 with the promise of a railroad. The railroad came the next year and ushered in prosperity. People flocked to the booming town, and numerous successful individuals and families constructed large homes and mansions. Life was good—until the Civil War started. *Above:* St. Luke's Episcopal Church was built in 1854 and served Cahawba until 1878, when the building was physically relocated to Martin's Station, about 15 miles away. The church remained active until 1901, when it closed. In 1936, the site was photographed during a historic building survey. It was later identified as a Cahawba church and in 2007 was moved back to Cahawba, where the building is currently undergoing restoration.

Left: Spanish moss drapes itself from the arms of a massive oak tree adjacent to the old W. W. and Elizabeth Fambro home. The house was built on a tall brick foundation that today is extremely unstable. The exact date of construction is not known, but it is assumed that Fambro built it in the early 1840s. A portion of the house appears older, indicating that this part may have been built earlier. Fambro, an attorney and the owner of a sawmill, lived there until he sold the 12-room home in 1853. It remained occupied until the late 1990s.

Auraria, Georgia

The ghost of Auraria hides in the wrinkled, corduroy piedmont at the southern end of the Appalachian Mountains in northern Georgia, about seven miles southwest of Dahlonega and 60 miles north of Atlanta. Today's Auraria is nothing like 1830s Auraria, when the booming gold-mining town had a weekly newspaper, *The Western Herald*, as well as enough saloons, hotels, and other businesses to supply the needs of 1,000 miners and other camp hangers-on.

Gold was discovered here around 1828, igniting the Georgia Gold Rush the following year. For the next 20 years, this region was the place to be, an area where towns popped up like mushrooms on a wet lawn. Auraria boomed quickly, challenging Dahlonega for the county seat. Dahlonega won and grew, and Auraria slowly faded through the 1830s and was almost completely depopulated when news of the California Gold Rush reached the mines of Georgia in 1848.

Having lost its will to live, with the farming capabilities in the area being recognized as poor and with few miners remaining, Auraria turned up its boots, laid down, and died. Today, the old Woody's Store building, Graham Hotel, and a few homes are all that remain. Those and memories of the days of old, days of gold, days of '29!

Above: Located at the junction of Auraria Road and Castleberry Bridge Road about seven miles southwest of Dahlonega, Woody's Store began life as a tavern. Today, it is one of the last remnants of the old mining town of Auraria. Prior to closing in the 1980s, this old general store served the community for many years after the gold rush was pushed into the recesses of history. The site of the wooden, two-story, Graham Hotel is located in the trees just to the left of the store. Long abandoned, the hotel collapsed a few years ago. Across the street is the site of an old bank. *Left:* Scattered about the area are numerous old cabins and homes dating back to the 19th century.

Georgia Gold Rush— The Dahlonega Mint

GOLD WAS KNOWN to exist in the eastern United States from the earliest days of colonization, but it took the discovery of a large nugget in North Carolina in 1799 to make the reality of that fact clear. Once that nugget was identified and the place where it was found successfully mined, folks listened to the old rumors of gold in the Georgia Mountains.

In 1828, the elusive yellow metal was discovered there, as well. Word spread, and in 1829, thousands of would-be miners converged on the northern Georgia mountain town of Dahlonega, spreading afield, seeking—and finding—gold. Headlines popped up, more miners arrived, and America's first gold rush was underway. Hundreds of small mining camps were established in the gold fields, camps that stretched southwest toward northern Alabama and northeast into the Carolina and Virginia Piedmont regions.

So much gold was found that the United States Mint established a branch mint at Dahlonega to make coins from it. The first of the mint's 1.4 mil-lion $1, $2.50 and $5 gold coins was struck on April 21, 1828. The mint closed on June 1, 1861, when Georgia seceded from the Union. The U.S. Treasury realized that there was no sense having a mint capable of producing coinage operating in enemy territory!

By the early 1840s, easy mining was over. Thousands of miners went back home, leaving behind America's first major cluster of ghost towns. The dying communities' position was cemented in 1848 when news of a gold strike in California created a mass exodus from the diminished gold fields of Georgia.

Above: Auraria and its remaining buildings have a fascinating story to tell. Some of the facts are about as elusive as clear title to land was in the 1830s, when the Cherokee were run off by encroaching miners. This red cabin is said to have been the homestead for Emory Brackett. Some call it Auraria's bank, but it appears that the bank was elsewhere. Another uncertainty is the naming of the town. According to the on-site historical monument, Auraria was named by U.S. Vice President John C. Calhoun, who also owned one of the earliest and richest gold mines to the east of town. Others, however, claim local citizen Major John Powell named the town.

In 1900 the Castleberry family of Auraria posed in this wagon being pulled by an ox.

Bulowville, Florida

Florida is an unlikely state in which to find ghost towns. At least, that's the popular misconception. In the Sunshine State, there are more than 300 of these old places hidden in the greenery, lost in the outback, or paved over, their sites bristling with tourist traps, mini malls, and subdivisions.

Bulowville is the ruin of an old sugar plantation "village" plopped along the upper east coast of Florida, just shy of 20 miles north of Daytona Beach. It is tucked under the trees at the north end of Bulow Creek State Park, on the south side of a mobile home park. Ruins remain of the plantation owner's mansion, well, boat docks, spring house, and sugar mill, as well as of coquina shell limestone foundations for some of the 46 12-foot by 16-foot slave houses.

Charles W. Bulow and his son John established this plantation, the largest sugar mill in Florida, in 1821. They cleared the land, planted the sugarcane in January and February, and harvested the crop in late October. Some 150 to 300 slave workers cut the cane, loaded it onto carts, and hauled it to the mill where it was rendered. Cotton, indigo, and rice were also raised in this self-sufficient little village.

In January 1836, during the 2nd Seminole War, the Seminole burned 16 plantations, including this one. It was never rebuilt, and today the ruins are a state historic park.

A VICTIM OF ITS TIMES

Built on coquina shell limestone, these rock ruins are all that remain of the former sugar mill at Bulowville. Charles Bulow established the plantation and built the sugar plant. After he died in 1823, his son, John, came home from Paris, France, to take over the family business. The mill thrived, and so did John Bulow. He had befriended the Seminole, becoming an out-spoken critic of the government's relocation plan for them. In 1836, a small state militia marched on Bulowville, and Bulow fired an empty cannon at the soldiers. They captured Bulow and the plantation, using it for forays against the Seminole. The poorly trained militia didn't do well, however, so it retreated to St. Augustine with Bulow still a prisoner. The Seminole burned Bulowville and other plantations in retribution. Once released, John Bulow returned to the charred ruins of his beloved home. Broken and dispirited, 27-year-old John Bulow returned to Paris, where he died a short time later.

Left: The fire-scarred ruins of the 119-foot by 93-foot steam powered sugar mill still stand in mute testimony to this once-bustling little community. It was the largest sugar mill in northeastern Florida during its day. About seven tons of cane were necessary to produce one ton of sugar. Because the process was so labor-intensive, Bulow had a large number of slaves to do the work. After the sugarcane was rendered into sugar and molasses, it was put in barrels and shipped via flatboats down Bulow Creek to outside markets.

Top: The now-peaceful site of the Bulowville Mansion belies the violence that gripped this historic plantation village in 1836. The wooden mansion was the heart of the Bulow sugar plantation. After Charles Bulow died and his son, John, took over, the mansion became the scene of many well-attended social events, attracting rich and well-known people. John James Audubon was one such visitor during Christmas week 1831. *Above:* This etched stone is from the boiler room wall of the sugar mill.

Alaska is blessed with some of the most beautiful scenery in the world, as well as some of the finest ghost town ruins. Rickety old mining structures such as Independence Mine remain scattered throughout the outback, while the dead supporting towns sit nearby. Because of the brutal Alaskan winters, once these mines closed, the towns died quickly and were often left to the elements. This was a hard life, and very few of these one-economy towns survived once that economic base crumbled.

Hawaii, Alaska, and Western Canada

These may be three seemingly unrelated areas, but one similarity they share is that they are ripe with ghost towns, including one of the most unique ghost towns in the world.

The Great Pacific

Hawaii is one of America's prime vacation spots, but very few of the visitors there know about the 50th state's ghost towns. Beginning in the mid-1800s and continuing through the 1900s, the sugar industry gave rise to company-owned towns supporting plantations and mills on the islands. Some of these mills operated until the early 2000s, although most had previously closed. Sugarcane was first grown commercially in 1835, with the peak years of production running from the 1920s through the early 1990s.

In addition to the company-owned sugar towns, two other creators of ghost towns were environmental—slow, viscous, flowing lava and a tsunami. Over the years, a number of towns on the Big Island of Hawaii have been destroyed by lava flows, including several in 1960 and more again around 1990. Ruins also remain of a number of coastal communities slammed by a tsunami generated by an 8.1-magnitude earthquake at Alaska's Aleutian island of Unimak on April 1, 1946. The 36-foot tsunami that struck the Hawaiian Islands around 7:00 A.M. was one of the most severe to ever strike the islands, causing millions of dollars in damage and killing 159 people in and around Hilo. Some of the seriously damaged coastal towns were never rebuilt. Hawaii also plays host to a pair of unique ghost towns, which were former centers for sufferers of Hansen's disease (for thousands of years known as leprosy).

The Alaskan Peninsula

North to Alaska, America's last frontier has a huge collection of old mining towns, remnants of the late 19th- and early 20th-century gold rushes that rocked the then territory. Beginning around 1880 at Juneau, prospectors roamed the massive territory for gold, making discoveries at Fortymile in 1886, on the Kenai Peninsula at Hope in 1893, and at Nome in 1898. These early rushes were eclipsed by the discovery of gold in Canada's Yukon Territory in 1896. Although not in Alaska, this discovery affected the future state, as the main port of entry for the Yukon mines was at the head of the Lynn Canal at the north end of the panhandle. Skagway and Dyea quickly developed into entrances into the backcountry. These two towns are where the 96ers would supply themselves with provisions and begin their brutal 550-mile overland trek up and over Chilkoot Pass and on to Dawson City.

The Alaska-Yukon Gold Rush focused prospectors on Alaska's interior. As mining spread, towns developed, flourished, and then died as the miners moved on. Today many of these old towns are just barely clinging to life. Many of the dead ones are forgotten. Some are accessible, but Alaskan highways are few, and distances are vast.

The Great White North

America's northern neighbor, Canada, is a huge country. Like the United States, it has thousands of ghost towns stretching coast to coast. The great Alaska-Yukon Gold Rush of 1896 focused the attention of the world on Canada's northwest.

Scores of thousands of miners trekked into the rugged region, opening up the vast interior of Alaska and northwestern Canada. Mining towns sprouted and withered, and Dawson City became a household name. This last great gold rush gave the world Sourdoughs, Cheechakos, and Jack London. Even Arizona legend Wyatt Earp ventured up here.

Down in the wide-open plains east of Alberta's Rocky Mountains, coal miners poked holes into the Canadian prairie, giving birth to mining towns that followed the typical cycle, fading in the mid-1900s. Several major clusters of mining towns popped up along the east side of the mountains west of Edmonton, west of Calgary. Another large group plopped down in the middle of the Crowsnest Pass area south of Calgary and just north of the U.S./Canada border at Waterton Lakes National Park. In the early 1900s, another cluster of small coal camps popped up in the Drumheller Valley area southeast of Calgary. Most of these old coal camps are now only memories, but quite a few still have viable remains, including the massive Atlas Mine coal tipple.

On the west side of the Rockies, British Columbia has a virtual smorgasbord of ghost towns of many varieties. Here industries such as mining, fishing, the military, and railroads built, nourished, and supported flourishing towns. But the pattern is clear by now: As the industries faded, the towns died.

During the 1860s, gold mining gave rise to numerous mining towns, one of which, Barkerville, is a grand example of the genre. Today, this restored mining town is a provincial park sharing the shining story of the Cariboo Gold Rush. Other mining towns lie throughout the interior, relics of the mid-century Fraser and Peace River rushes.

Along the Pacific Coast, fishing villages and other points of civilization boomed and faded. Fur, agriculture, lumber, and mining gained in importance. As British Columbia gained notoriety, it was added to the expanding nation of Canada as a province in 1871. The military also established a number of forts for protection, some of which became small self-sufficient communities.

Today the relics of Hawaii's company-owned sugar towns draw tourists. Alaska's gold rush heritage is celebrated, and the entire state still reaps the rewards of the great gold rush, as does Canada's Yukon Territory and Dawson City. The former coal camps of Alberta have faded, their bustling streets now deserted, while the old ghosts of British Columbia quietly bask in the glory of days past.

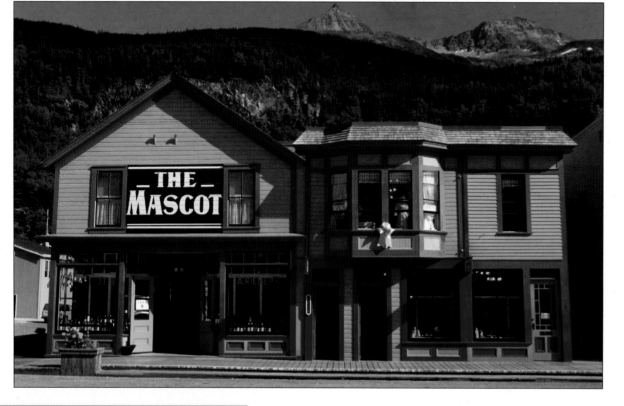

Sometimes pioneering towns were situated in strategic locations, so once the boom that created them subsided, the towns remained alive, albeit much smaller than during the boom days. Over the years, their century-old buildings have been restored, repainted, and repurposed, as has happened with The Mascot in Skagway, Alaska.

Due to isolation and long travel distances from product markets, old mining towns in the Alaskan backcountry required self-sufficiency. Complete towns were built up around the mines, and huge mills cascaded down the sides of hills, such as the Kennecott Mining Company Mill does here. Built of easily obtainable wood, these massive complexes often towered over the supporting community. Yet size doesn't always matter. Once the ore ran out or became unprofitable to mine, the mine closed, the mill shut down, and the people caught the last train out.

Leper Colonies of Hawaii

The person who has the leprous disease shall wear torn clothes and let the hair of his head be dishevelled; and he shall cover his upper lip and cry out, "Unclean, unclean." He shall remain unclean as long as he has the disease; he is unclean. He shall live alone; his dwelling shall be outside the camp.

—Leviticus 13:45–46

This reference to infectious skin diseases from the Bible shows the history of human bias against persons afflicted with various contagious skin diseases, or skin-affecting diseases such as leprosy, now called Hansen's disease. Today, Hansen's disease is controllable by drugs, so it is not the scourge it once was.

This disease was introduced to the kingdom of Hawaii around 1848. Since there was no known treatment at that time, victims of the disease were exiled to the north side of the island of Molokai. In 1866, the Kalaupapa and Kalawao Leper Colonies were established to hold those with the disease in isolation.

In 1864, 24-year-old Father Damien (born Joseph de Veuster in Belgium) arrived in the Hawaiian Islands as a Catholic missionary. Seven years later, he asked his bishop to be transferred to the leper colonies so he could minister to the afflicted residents there. For 16 years, he provided compassionate care and spiritual guidance for the residents of the two colonies. Then on April 15, 1889, Father Damien died, a victim of that very disease.

In 1980, Kalaupapa and Kalawao became a national historic park due to their importance to both Hawaiian and American history.

United States Leprosarium on Molokai, Hawaii.

Top: When Belgian-born Catholic priest Father Damien went to the Kalaupapa and Kalawao Leper Colonies willingly, he knew the risks. He spent the rest of his life ministering to the residents. On Sunday, October 11, 2009, Father Damien's work at the colony was recognized when he was canonized by Pope Benedict XVI, who elevated the humble priest to sainthood. *Above:* This old postcard displays the massive sea cliffs that isolated the United States Leprosarium from the rest of the island.

Top: Beautiful old Saint Philomena Catholic Church stands along the road to Kalawao, greeting visitors as it has since 1872 when it was a small wooden chapel. When Father Damien arrived at Kalaupapa and Kalawao, he spent his first nights here, sleeping under a tree next to the chapel. Father Damien expanded the building twice, situating it to take advantage of cooling winds that blew through open windows and having parishioners paint the interior in bright, cheerful colors. Father Damien's grave is located here, where a black cross marks his former burial site. *Above:* Abandoned homes such as this once housed the former residents of the Kalaupapa community.

The Hawaiian Sugar Industry

Hawaii is known for many things, including sun, sand, leis, luaus, tourism, pineapples, and sugar. Regarding the latter, the popular television commercial jingles touting C&H Sugar Company's "pure cane sugar from Hawaii" became ingrained in an earlier generation of Americans.

The California & Hawaii Sugar Company (C&H) was just one of many sugar-producing companies tapping Hawaii's perfect sugarcane growing climate to provide for the world's sweet tooth. The industry began on the islands in 1834, and as it took hold, much of the area was covered with sugar plantations, sugar mills, and sugar shipping ports, along with their ubiquitous supporting towns. As the sugar companies signed leases from Hawaiian royalty, the companies provided needed revenue for the government. In turn, this increased the importance of Hawaii as the sugar industry became the dominant industry on the islands.

By the time Hawaii became a state in 1959, nearly 10 percent of the population was employed in the sugar industry. As tourism has increased, sugar plantations have slowly closed, and the number of plantations has dropped dramatically. From its peak in the early 1930s, the industry saw a major collapse from the 1960s through the 1990s. In 2009, only two plantations remained, one of which was scheduled to close in mid-2010. Today, skeletons of the old sugar towns lie scattered across the islands. Now-abandoned mills, plantation ruins, and dead wharves at Honuapo, Koloa, Kualoa, and Waialua hearken back to the boom days of Hawaii's white gold.

Independence Mine, Alaska

Six million dollars—that's the reported production from the Independence Mine located in Hatcher Pass, about 16 air miles north of Wasilla, Alaska. This mine and its wonderfully picturesque ruins are relics of the mid-20th century.

The original gold in Hatcher Pass was discovered in 1906 by Robert Hatcher. The Alaska Gold Quartz Mining Company staked its claims in 1907 but did not do any serious work until the late 1930s. From 1937 until the mine was closed in 1942, the Independence Mine, with 200 employees, was one of the busiest mines in the district. The mining camp located below it had more than two dozen buildings, including an apartment house, two bunkhouses, a cookhouse/mess hall, a combination commissary/post office/mining office, an assay office, an electrical shop, a machine shop, a mill building, a powerhouse, a framing shop, stores of all kinds, and about 20 individual cabins for married miners and their families.

After the end of World War II, the mine reopened and operated until January 1951, when it shut down for good. In 1974, the historical value of the property was noted, and it was listed on the National Register of Historic Places. In 1980, the owners donated it to the state of Alaska, and Independence Mine State Historic Park was formed. Since then, some of the buildings have been restored, and others have been stabilized.

These proud miners from the first half of the 1900s stand at a windlass, a winch used to lower and raise materials into and out of the mine.

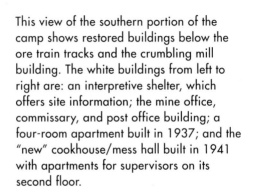

This view of the southern portion of the camp shows restored buildings below the ore train tracks and the crumbling mill building. The white buildings from left to right are: an interpretive shelter, which offers site information; the mine office, commissary, and post office building; a four-room apartment built in 1937; and the "new" cookhouse/mess hall built in 1941 with apartments for supervisors on its second floor.

Viewed from below, the massive mill and associated support buildings lie mostly in a heap of tossed wood flotsam, victims of neglect and heavy snow.

REMNANTS OF A NORTHERN COMPANY TOWN

The northern portion of the mining camp includes a cluster of larger buildings. The first floor of the big, white, three-story building on the left housed the engineering offices and a warehouse (which stocked all the needed supplies for the crew). The second and third floors held bunk rooms, one of which was used as a school for a short time. The three-story building to the rear center was Bunkhouse #1, which was built in 1938 and housed 50 people. This building had electricity, plumbing, and heating. The smaller building in the center was a framing shop. Here large timbers were cut for mine supports. It also supplied lumber used for construction jobs around the camp. Just out of sight to the left was Bunkhouse #2. At the time the mining camp and its facilities were established, they were state-of-the-art and provided better accommodations than most of the miners were used to.

Kennicott, Alaska

Is it spelled with an *I* or an *E*? The parent company, Kennecott Mines Company, spells it with an *E*. The mining camp was named after a nearby glacier, which was named after naturalist and explorer Robert Kennicott, and is spelled with an *I*. Still in business and based in Utah, the Kennecott Mining Company was also named after him, even though it is spelled differently.

From 1906 through 1938, this copper mining town was located at the foot of the Wrangell Range in the southeast corner of nonpanhandle Alaska, an isolated area. Mining began around 1906, and in 1908 the post office was established, along with a train to Cordova, the Copper River & Northwestern Railway. The mining camp had 494 people in 1920 and at its peak is said to have had 800 folks. As a remote company town, Kennicott had to be self-sufficient, so among its amenities were a hospital, a movie theater, a recreation hall, and a school. It also had a clean reputation with strict rules for citizens to follow. In December 1938, the post office closed, the residents boarded the last train out of Kennicott, and the town was abandoned.

In 1941, the Kennecott Company deeded the railroad to the state for use as a road. Except for a few curious and adventurous types who managed to work their way into town, the old mining camp sat vacant. Then in 1986, it was declared a national historic landmark. The National Park Service has come in and is in the process of restoring some of the 40 buildings that remain.

Left: A three-story boarding house at Kennicott's Jumbo Mine is about to tip over. Because of neglect between the years when the camp was abandoned and when the National Park Service took over, numerous buildings in the old mining town have become unstable and thus unsafe to enter. *Above:* This sign tells it all. Guided tours are offered of the facilities in Kennicott, which allows access to some of the closed areas. *Below:* Visible in the mill complex are buildings that housed the leaching plant (*left*), the machine shop (*center*), and the concentration mill (*right*).

Opposite page: Despite its advancing state of ruin, the abandoned mill building ascending the hill behind the desolate copper-mining town of Kennicott remains an imposing sight. *Above:* This July 1982 view of Kennicott's power plant building looks to the northeast. The plant supplied electrical power to the massive mill complex as well as to the town.

Skagway, Alaska

They came, they saw, they went. Treasure seekers hustled off of all types of floating vessels that got them to the wooden docks extending out into the mud-flats at Skagway. Bright lights, cards, booze, and female companionship beckoned, trying to separate them from what little money they had. Inflated prices and the Canadian requirement that miners carry massive supply loads slapped the new arrivals with reality. Skagway was willing to cooperate—for a price.

Established at the head of the Inside Passage, Skagway was not a mining town but was instead an outfitting center and gathering point for miners during the great Klondike Gold Rush of 1897–98. This was just the beginning of the grueling 450-mile overland trail to the Yukon's gold mines around Dawson City. Within a year of the first boat's landing in July 1897, Skagway had become Alaska's largest city, with upwards of 10,000 people. Gold, lawlessness, and anarchy made it famous, and tourism has kept it alive.

After the gold rush, Skagway faded but didn't die. In 1900, as many as 1,800 people remained, and the population has not ducked below 500 since. Gone were the boomers, gone were the saloons, and gone were the diversions. Post-boom Skagway capitalized on its location, remaining a shipping center for inland mines as well as being a popular cruise ship destination and tourist center. This quaint little town filled with Victorian buildings and 862 residents annually draws more than 900,000 folks looking to experience its colorful gold-rush past.

Above: No longer catering to sourdoughs readying themselves for the long trek to the frozen north along the Yukon River, Skagway's Golden North Hotel now welcomes modern visitors. It was built in 1898 as a two-story hotel and, in 1908, was moved to its present location. The third floor and golden "onion dome" were added at that time. This is Alaska's oldest still-operating hotel. *Left:* In the "good old days" of the gold rush, Skagway's streets were an unending parade of miners heading off to the hinterlands. This was their last chance to stock up on the massive amounts of provisions required by Canadian officials before entering Canada. Drugstores, hardware stores, general stores, and outfitting companies competed with each other for the miners' business, while on the backstreets, less upstanding businesses also flourished.

Above left: Skagway's Gold Rush cemetery was the last resting place for many miners who never made it beyond the diversions offered in town. Jefferson Randolph "Soapy" Smith II, a gold rush–era con artist, saloon owner, and ring leader of crime in and around Skagway, is interred here, as is Frank Reid, one of his victims. When Reid went, however, he didn't go alone. He and Soapy killed each other in a July 8, 1898, shoot-out. Soapy died instantly, whereas Reid lingered for 12 days before passing. Tombstones visible here include Reid's and one for Carolina Hilly. Above: This relocated and restored 350-ton, 1937 gold dredge is located on the Skagway River just outside town. Gold mining did not occur at Skagway, but the dredge was brought in from the Klondike area in 1999 to represent a little of that facet of the mining industry.

Above: These restored buildings are part of Skagway's "Old Town." Right: This unique driftwood facade welcomes visitors to the Arctic Brotherhood's "Camp Skagway No 1" building in downtown Skagway. The Arctic Brotherhood was a fraternal order organized by 11 Skagway-bound men in February 1899 to provide mutual support, aid, and friendship in Alaska and the Yukon mines.

Dawson City, Yukon Territory

It has been called the Last Great Gold Rush. In August 1896, gold was discovered near the confluence of the Klondike and Yukon rivers in the heart of Canada's Yukon Territory, seemingly a gazillion miles from anywhere and everywhere. Once word hit Seattle in the summer of 1897, as many as 100,000 starry-eyed miners and wannabe miners converged to this point on the Yukon River. Unfortunately for them, all the best locations had already been staked, and mining had commenced. They persisted, however, and the summers of 1897 and 1898 were like the California Gold Rush revisited.

Most came by sea through Skagway and its neighboring town of Dyea, so after the brutal 450-mile journey to Dawson City, they had to make the best of the situation. Dawson blossomed in the long summer days, and soon some 25,000 to 40,000 people called it home. Grand Forks, ten miles south on Bonanza Creek, had 10,000 residents. Neither of those numbers includes the thousands living outside the grasp of those two towns. By 1898, Dawson had reached its peak and had bustling suburbs at Klondike City and Grand Forks.

Dawson City was no shrinking violet and gave Skagway a run for its money on prices, vices, and corruption. The flush years didn't last long, however. By 1899 the population had dropped by 8,000, and then to 5,000 by the time Dawson incorporated in 1902. In 2006, the census counted 1,327 people, most earning their living mining gold or catering to the 60,000 tourists a year that explore its historic streets.

Top: Stacks of firewood, dog teams, and snow-covered mountains in the background show that Dawson City was not your everyday mining town. *Above:* Ripped apart by four fires in its first four years and built alongside the Yukon River on permafrost, Dawson City still lives on. The miners are mostly gone, as are the stacks of firewood and the dog teams.

A bakery and ice cream shop decorate restored, painted storefronts of today's Dawson City. A deep pride of the past and a tough development policy, as well as a town ordinance that requires all new or remodeled buildings to be built in the style of the old town, keeps the community looking similar to the way it did more than 100 years ago.

Located at the corner of 2nd Avenue and Queen, the Downtown Hotel is actually the replacement for the original, which was built in 1902 and was renowned for its service and hospitality. The first building was destroyed by fire in 1980. The current hotel was built in 1981 and 1982 on the original site and was remodeled in 2002. It continues to serve visitors to this far north town.

Klondike Gold Rush

GOLD! THAT WORD pasted onto the front pages of newspapers has changed world history. In 1828, it was Georgia; in 1848, California. In 1851, gold fever crossed the Pacific to Australia, then to South Africa in the 1880s. After several minor flurries of excitement in Alaska, the jackpot was hit along Canada's Yukon River in 1896. Some 100,000 people headed for the Klondike and Yukon rivers near Dawson City for a couple years of rollicking times. The Klondike Gold Rush was the last hurrah, one final gold rush galvanizing the world, ending America and Canada's Wild West period.

Klondike Fever began in mid-1897 at the Port of Seattle when a couple of docking ships brought news of rich gold discoveries, as well as bagged proof. Word spread rapidly and, as in previous gold rushes, enticed many thousands of folks to respond.

This rush, however, was somewhat different than most of those previous, as it was located in an area that had brutally cold winters. In addition, Canadian authorities wouldn't allow miners into the area unless they brought a year's worth of supplies with them. Because of the Yukon's isolation, by the time most folks reached the gold mines, practically all the good claims were long gone. So, three choices presented themselves: work for others, prospect further into the wilderness, or return home. Decisions were made, and more gold was found. A number of mining camps and towns spread across the Yukon and Alaska territories, forever changing North America's map.

PAST AND PRESENT

This top overview of Dawson City was taken from Midnight Dome looking south. It shows the extent of the present town at the confluence of the Yukon and Klondike rivers. Most of the land on which Dawson is built is permafrost, which can play havoc on buildings during freeze-thaw cycles. The bottom picture, at a lower elevation, was taken in 1898 after the town had grown from virtually nothing to having a population of as many as 40,000 people. Two or three years earlier, this area had been a First Nations (Canadian native peoples) settlement.

Above left: Historic St. Mary's Catholic Church, shown here in the present day, dates to the early days of settlement. *Above:* The historic old paddle-wheel steamship S.S. *Keno* sits next to the abandoned Dawson City branch of the Canadian Bank of Commerce. The 130-foot *Keno* was built in 1922 and carried silver, lead, and zinc ore between Stewart and the Mayo Mining District until 1960. It was one of a fleet of 60 or more steamers that once plied the rivers in Alaska and the Yukon, delivering all the necessities of life to these remote towns. This bank building opened in 1898; by 1908, some $44 million in gold had been processed through it. The building has been closed for many years, sitting unused near the riverfront. *Left:* About ten years after the initial gold discovery in the Klondike, around 24 dredges began to work the rivers. This dredge, Number 4, was located along Bonanza Creek and operated until 1959. It is North America's largest wood-hulled bucket line dredge and is currently a Canada National Historic Site.

Barkerville, British Columbia

On the Cariboo Wagon Road, deep in the heart of British Columbia—55 miles east of Quesnel and southeast of Prince George—is the magnificent, restored ghost town of Barkerville. Billy Barker discovered gold on Williams Creek in 1862, and thousands of miners descended into the area around his claims. By the next summer, hotels, restaurants, cafés, saloons, dance halls, a church, a barbershop, and a multitude of stores lined the long main street of the new town of Barkerville, and some 10,000 people swarmed its sidewalks and streets.

But the compact wooden town was a fire waiting to happen. In September 1868, the wait was over. After the fire, Barkerville was quickly rebuilt—in wood—but with space for cross streets.

Barkerville was not a violent town, despite the gin mills, dance halls, and other such diversions. But by 1870, the end was near. As gold production decreased, other new booms elsewhere caught the attention of the miners, who abandoned Barkerville for more enticing opportunities.

In 1957, the province of British Columbia purchased this property and began to restore its buildings. Today, more than 125 buildings have been renewed, giving Barkerville a second life as a living history museum.

Above: Downtown Barkerville no longer bustles with miners and their daily commerce. To the left is the former government assay office and adjacent law offices. To the right is Kelly's General Store. *Left:* St. Saviour's Anglican Church is located at the northern end of this ghost town. Its doors opened on September 18, 1870, and services are still held during the summer tourist season. This church structure is one of the ghost town's most recognizable buildings.

Right: This photo was taken on Dominion Day (a holiday now known as Canada Day), July 1, 1871. The Barkerville library is on the left, with John and Emily Bowron standing out front. Next door, Mr. and Mrs. William Davison stand in the doorway of their grocery store. Note the elevated sidewalk.

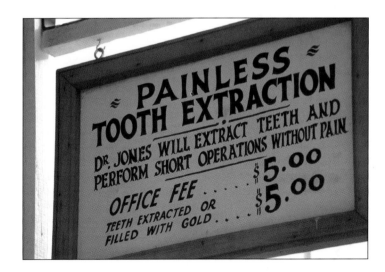

Above: The still-active Cariboo Lodge #4, Masonic Hall sits on the west side of the main street. The lodge dates to 1869, but this building is its third home, having been rebuilt after the fire of 1937. *Above right:* Wonder what Doctor Jones used for pain killer? That fact may be lost to history. *Right:* The old stove inside this Barkerville cabin probably spent many winter days glowing nearly red to beat back the heavy, damp cold of British Columbia's interior winter weather.

Fort Rodd Hill, British Columbia

One of the best preserved Canadian coastal defense fortifications is located just west of Victoria, on the south end of Vancouver Island. The Victoria-Esquimalt Fortress and Fisgard Lighthouse created a small community that protected the entrances to Victoria and Esquimalt harbors from all enemies. Like most coastal defense fortifications in the United States and Canada, the massive gun batteries were never fired in anger at any foreign enemy.

Built by the British, the Victoria-Esquimalt Fortress was in use by them between 1878 and 1906. It was then turned over to—and operated by—the Canadian military until 1956. Fort Rodd Hill is the best preserved of the forts in the Victoria-Esquimalt Fortress complex and is probably the best example of British Coastal Defense Forts in the world today. This fort has not been restored, recreated, or gussied up. The original structures have received very minor work.

The fort consisted of massive gun emplacements, some of whose guns were capable of firing 100-pound, six-inch shells a distance of six miles. Supporting buildings included barracks, underground ammunition bunkers, a canteen, command posts, guard houses, searchlight towers, a telephone exchange, and a 7,000-gallon water tank. Site-wide historical displays and signage explain the importance of the fort, bringing to life the experiences of those who once lived here.

Above: From the sea, Fisgard Lighthouse stands tall with Fort Rodd Hill directly behind it. The lighthouse was named for the British ship H.M.S. *Fisgard,* which was stationed in the region from 1844 through 1847. The lighthouse and the fort are historically independent of each other, although today they are administered together. *Left:* Built by the British, Fisgard Lighthouse stands on a spit jutting out into Esquimalt Harbour. It was the first permanent lighthouse on Canada's west coast. The light was lit on November 16, 1860, and it has been safely guiding ships into the harbor ever since. In 1928, the light was automated, so the lighthouse keeper and his family were no longer needed. They lived in the large brick house adjacent to the light tower. This photograph is likely from the 1950s.

This late 1950s view of Fort Rodd Hill shows the concrete wall protecting the rear flank along the land side of the stronghold. Fort Rodd Hill was unique for coastal defense forts in that, due to its isolation, it was completely surrounded by a wall. The rear-facing wall had gun slits in it to allow the occupants to defend themselves if necessary.

Built in 1897, this two-story brick building housed the married noncommissioned (NCO) and warrant officers. During its history, it also served as an officer's mess and a command post.

Dorothy and the Drumheller Valley, Alberta

The Drumheller Valley, 75 miles northeast of Calgary, is the heart of Alberta's badlands, a dry rolling landscape loaded with hoodoos, coulees, and numerous ghost and semi-ghost towns.

Cambria and Wayne are the shriveled remains of neighboring coal towns from the era between 1910 and 1940. At Cambria, a sign tells the story: "As work progressed the [coal] seam ran poorly as there was too much bone in the coal." Those bones were dinosaur bones! Wayne's buildings include the well-preserved Rosedeer Hotel and Last Chance Saloon.

Established in 1928, East Coulee only has about 5 percent of the population it had in the 1930s. Its coal mines closed by the late 1940s.

At the nearby Atlas Coal Mine, a 1918 list of its 52 miners looked like the United Nations: Canada was home to 15; England, 10; Italy, 9; Sweden, 5; Scotland, 4; United States, 3; and Belgium, France, Ireland, Norway, Russia, and Wales, 1 each. As Atlas was one of the last mines to close, most of the original buildings and machinery remain. This mine is located just a mile southeast of East Coulee.

A tad down the road from there is Dorothy. The Dorothy post office opened in this tiny agricultural community in 1908, and by the 1920s the railroad had come. Dorothy boasted of three grain elevators, a church, a school, a restaurant, a butcher shop, a pool room, and three stores all to serve the less than 100 residents. Most of those buildings remain—empty.

IN THE SHADOW OF THE ROCKY MOUNTAINS

Deep in the backcountry of Alberta, out among the coulees, is the tiny early 20th-century agricultural town of Dorothy. *Opposite page:* Two churches were established here, about a hundred yards apart, a United church (*right*) and a Roman Catholic church (*left*), shown here through the window of the United church building. Restoration of both buildings by the Dorothy Historical Society commenced around 2006 and is still ongoing. *Left:* W. G. Hodgson was a cowboy-rancher who gained international fame and critical acclaim as a carver of delicate wooden figurines using twisted, gnarled juniper roots as his medium and homemade implements built of automobile parts as his carving tools. His art was mentioned in a 1934 article in Popular Mechanics. He lived in this house in Dorothy, photographed circa 1948. *Below right:* The sole survivor of the three grain elevators that once lined the railroad tracks at Dorothy is the Alberta Pacific Grain Company Limited grain elevator. Today the tracks are gone, as is the prosperity of this once-busy, little agricultural community. *Below:* In 1952, a cable ferry still carried cars across the Red Deer River. Dorothy and a pair of grain elevators are visible on the far side of the river.

Index